THE JO
STAM

Hunter Davies is the author of twenty-five books; he is also a contributor to *Punch* magazine, where his column 'Father's Day' appears regularly, to the *Sunday Times* (ex-Atticus) and to *Stamp and Postal History News*. He is married to the writer Margaret Forster, and they have three children and every lavatory decorated with his stamps.

Some Historical Dates
1660

Act of Parliament in the reign of Charles II establishes the General Post Office.

1784

First mail coach service gets underway — between London and Bristol via Bath.

1830

The Post Office sees the advantages of the new railways and uses the Manchester and Liverpool Railway for the first railborne mail in the world.

1840

Rowland Hill introduces his reforms. Rates are calculated on weight and the new minimum is a penny, paid by the sender who purchases the stamp to stick on the letter as proof of having paid.

1883

Parcel post is born. Before this, people had to rely on their own resources.

1911

World's first scheduled airmail service, 9–16 September. Planes carry special 'Aerial Post' between Hendon and Windsor as part of the Coronation celebrations of King George V.

1984

The Joy of Stamps is published.

THE JOY OF STAMPS

HUNTER DAVIES

With cartoons by Gordon Stowell

 Robson Books

The author wishes to thank *Stamp and Postal History News* for permission to include material previously published by them. Many of the cartoons in this book also appeared there, and are reproduced by permission.

FIRST PUBLISHED IN GREAT BRITAIN IN HARD-BACK IN 1983 BY ROBSON BOOKS LTD., BOLSOVER HOUSE, 5-6 CLIPSTONE STREET, LONDON W1P 7EB. THIS ROBSON PAPERBACK EDITION FIRST PUBLISHED IN 1984. COPYRIGHT © 1983 HUNTER DAVIES

British Library Cataloguing in Publication Data

Davies, Hunter
    The joy of stamps
    1. Postage-stamps
    Collectors and collecting – anecdotes, facetiae, satire etc.
    I. Title
    769.56'075 HE6213

ISBN 0-86051-285-1

Printed in Hungary

Introduction

This is a story of an ordinary stamp collector which I hope will appeal to ordinary stamp collectors everywhere.

There are said to be at least two million collectors out there somewhere, gazing at our treasures, lost in our reveries — perhaps even four million, depending on whom you believe. The stamp industry as a whole is not well organised and there are conflicting figures and conflicting definitions. We all agree, however, that we are part of the World's Greatest Hobby. More people collect stamps than collect anything else. Hurray for philately.

But who wants to read about an *ordinary* collector? Good question. After all Stanley Gibbons, the world's leading stamp dealer, is stuffed with experts, as are Sotheby's and the other famous auction houses, all of whom employ very knowledgeable stamp people. As for the stamp press, its pages are filled with perfectly formed philatelic prose, carefully carved out by the leaders of our distinguished philatelic societies and organisations. An outsider should step warily.

The first answer is that collecting stamps is a *hobby*. Only the dealers and such-like do it professionally. The rest of us do it in the margins of our life. We are all ordinary collectors. Secondly, as an ordinary collector I find stamps both fun and funny and I have tried to write accordingly.

The other day I met Basil Boothroyd, who has graced the pages of *Punch* for many years, and he asked me what I was doing. I muttered a few things, listed my latest prospects, including a so-called funny column about stamps. He stopped in his tracks. 'Dear boy, it must be a one-off.'

I started writing about stamps in 1980, so you can see what an outsider I am, soon after I had begun to collect stamps. It was something I had not done since boyhood. For about thirty years I had not only ignored stamps, I treated collectors as joke figures, not worth taking seriously, obviously deprived, compensating for something unmentionable, pathetic specimens with their pathetic specimens. I used collecting stamps as my ultimate example of boringness, rating it only one step up from fretwork.

Now, just three years later, I find it hard to understand what has happened to me, what strange event has taken over my life. We all have an image of ourselves, usually wrong, and in my version of myself I am all action and movement, rushing around in a mad panic, doing too many things at the same time. Today, I sometimes look up, when the days have been flashing past, and think where am I, what am I doing. My eyes ache with peering through my magnifying glass and my fingers lie limp from clutching the tweezers.

I am trying at present to ration myself, to go on a diet, give myself a stamp-free week in which I promise not to touch one till I have done some proper work, saving them up like a pudding. They do make perfect afters, treats for good behaviour, though at other times they almost drive me crazy. I do get high on the joy of stamps, as you will see, but I also become fed up and decide the whole thing is ridiculous. Till the next post comes.

I had just begun this madness, and had mentioned it in passing in various articles or books, thinking that nobody out there was at all interested, which is what most stamp collectors have to suffer, when in early 1981 I got a call from a gentleman called Irwin Margolis who said he was beginning a stamp newspaper, the country's first. He asked me to write a personal column, similar to the 'Father's Day' column I do in *Punch*. Instead of rambling on about my family, I could ramble on about my stamps. I jumped. (I also happen to be Philatelic Correspondent of *The Sunday Times*, a job I created for myself, having worked for the paper in other capacities for over twenty years. I thought the visiting cards would come in handy when trying to impress the stamp trade. Perhaps even get me a few discounts. Fat chance.)

Looking back through all I've written for *Stamp and Postal History News*, it forms a sort of narrative. We can see the virgin collector in the early stages of his passion, carried away with silly things, like railway stamps and Penny Reds. He falls in love with a local stamp shop, till something tragic happens to make him change his habits. As the months go on, his collection expands, new specialities emerge, old ones fade, more knowledge comes in — or so he likes to think — and more money goes out, though he likes to think not.

There are ups and downs, good times and bad. He goes to stamp exhibitions, discovers street stalls, decides to begin his own stamp fair, visits a stamp club, tries and fails to sell his swops.

All the ordinary things which ordinary collectors will understand.

I began my obsession in 1979, at the height of the most recent stamp boom, an unlucky time to start as the prices have since fallen — much to my fury. This probably explains why I feel as though I'm always moaning about dealers, though I have in fact come to understand their problems a little better. But as an ordinary collector I still feel I should write about it from our side, not from their side. They are in it as a business. We are in it for fun. I have had four years so far. I hope you enjoy this account of them.

July 1983

Yours in stamps
Hunter Davies
London NW5

First Day Covers

When I was young, I used to be passionate about them, always trying to add to my collection. It's strange how for a time one can be obsessed, able to think of nothing else, when a sort of madness takes over one's whole being and one's whole body. Ah, what joys, the bliss of youth, when it all seemed so simple and uncomplicated. Fade, sweet music, soft lights, here we go down memory lane.

I always wanted them in mint condition in those days, pure and virginal, unsoiled by any other hands. I refused to even consider any of those tasty ones, examples which had been around, passed from one to another. Only the best was good enough. What standard I had in those far-off days.

Now, I rather prefer them when they've seen a bit of service, taken a few interesting knocks and bashes. You can tell so much from their markings, from their blemishes, how at some stage someone has tried a bit of repair work to the face, or done some clever disguising on the rear. Every wrinkle tells a story, so they say. Mind you, no one wants them in rotten condition, all frayed at the edges, poor colour, torn and faded. I do like to see a good profile.

In those days, I always went for British ones. I never fancied those foreigners, strange examples from exotic overseas countries. Perhaps I was frightened, scared to commit myself, to become entangled with something I might not be able to handle with my tweezers. I did go through a phase of liking letters in French, but that did not last long.

I hated it when other boys made disgusting references to examples I was fond of, ran them down, made rude remarks, suggested all was not as it appeared to me. I accused them of being jealous. I was proud of my hobby, and refused to listen to their nasty comments.

I used to hang around Church Halls a lot, hoping to pick up something new and exciting, poking around, looking at what was on offer, but very often when I got them home I used to regret what I had done, realising I had paid too high a price. It's funny how you can get carried away, taken in by a flashy set, over-impressed by a good looker.

I did little mounting in those days. I was of course very young. This must have been back in the 1950s. We did not have the advantage of all the modern devices collectors have today

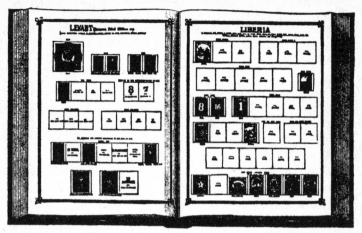

FIG. I.—Fully Printed Album ("Ideal").

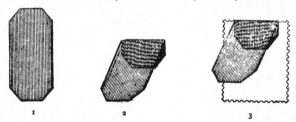

FIG. P.—(1) The hinge; (2) folded; (3) affixed to back of stamp ready for mounting in album.

which make the hobby so much easier to handle. I remember when those smooth, transparent things first came in from Sweden. What excitement. It seemed it would solve all our problems and change our lives, but of course, nothing really altered in the end. Good examples, in tip-top condition, were just as hard to get hold of as they ever had been.

For a while, as I got older, I progressed to hotels, to meeting in overheated back rooms with thick pile carpets. There was often a much better type available there, better laid out and well presented, but it always seemed to be much more expensive. At heart, I always preferred it out in the open air, on a village green, or even in the street. For the rougher sort of trade, a lot of boys used to go to Fairs, but I kept away from such places. I was scared I might pick up the wrong sort, the fakes and the forgeries, the gutter types.

I preferred the classic beauties, the straightforward, clean specimens. I know there were boys who went for the unusual things like re-entries, which I never understood, but always suspected, or plating which sounded horrid or went for pairs or even specialised in multiples and did strange things with miniature sheets. None of that was for me. But, as I say, I was young in those days.

There were a few clubs where boys with similar interests would gather and exchange names and numbers, good addresses, and give each other hints and advice. Some even prepared their own exhibitions. Others swopped, passing on details of ones they had finished with. I kept out of all that; I liked the chase best, hunting them down on my own, the excitement of suddenly seeing something new and working out ways of capturing it.

It did make for rather a lonely hobby at times. At school, I was often reprimanded for looking at them when I should have been working, hiding them under my desk, ogling them when the lesson was dull or my mind had wandered. It seemed such an all-consuming pastime, back in those far-off days.

Eventually, when I reached about sixteen, the passion began to ease somewhat. I think by eighteen I had given up girls completely. That was when I decided to take up stamps . . .

The Universal Postal Union was made worldwide in 1863 at the Paris Postal Conference. It now contains virtually every postal administration in the world and is the only international body to have continued to operate during the two World Wars.

The story so far. It was Christmas in my workhouse and my wife gave me a stamp album as a present. I suppose I must have mentioned that I might collect stamps again, one of these days. I did collect them as a boy, for all of ten minutes, or perhaps fifteen, then quickly gave them up and moved on to girls. They weren't as easy to collect as they are today, but they seemed much more fun than stamps. At the time. Now, I'm back to stamps. Much more interesting.

I was given this album for Christmas 1979, though it seems like a hundred years ago. I started with railway stamps, as I've always been interested in railways, and I bought one of those packets you see everywhere, a hundred railway stamps for £1.25, all different.

It seemed a bargain at the time, and I carefully checked to make sure each was different. What I wasn't able to check, being such a novice, was if they were any good. Now I know most were a load of rubbish. To think I even cleared a space in my precious new Stanley Gibbons album for a sheet of junk from some place called Umm Al Qaiwan, wherever that is, even if it did have some trains on it.

" I think it all started when I began collecting famous people on stamps."

I've probably got about two thousand railway stamps now. Going backwards is good fun, trying to get copies of the earliest trains on stamps, such as the USA three-cent blue 1869, but the present day is a big bore. In fact present-day stamps drive me round the bend.

I made the mistake of circulating lots of dealers, when I'd just begun, and now they keep sending me all this stuff from countries I'm sure don't exist. They also insist on sending me stamps issued by the Preserved Railway companies. Now, I'm all for preserved railways, some of my best friends and I know they need the money, but I don't want their stamps. Thank you, no. They're just labels. I am a serious railway stamp collector, don't you know?

Then I bought a Penny Black for £25 from a man on a stall in a market. A serious stamp collector should have a Penny Black, after all. I looked it up in my Gibbons' *Stamps of the World* and it said a mint one was worth £2,000 and a used one £125. What a bargain. Clever old me. I rushed down to Gibbons in the Strand and they said go away, you dumdum, it's worth £5 at the most.

I'm quite fond of it now, poor, sad specimen that it is, all faded and tatty, only one margin to its name, probably not even got OG, if I knew how to detect OG. One thing about collecting bad stamps is that you soon learn how to recognise bad stamps.

I am now well on the way to collecting one of every Victorian stamp, though there are quite a few spaces in my album. You must not have spaces, of course, judging by all that brain-washing which the dealers try to inflict upon us in the stamp press. Cover up those unsightly gaps. You feel as if you've got leprosy.

I now have quite a few other collections, *culs de sac* which I've wandered into, which I will tell you about later, or moan about probably. So far, I've had endless pleasure out of stamps, and I can think of no other hobby which is so harmless, so easy to organise, so neat and tidy, which upsets nobody else and doesn't frighten the horses but – gee whiz – I often sit there and scream inwardly to myself as I look at the latest catalogues. There is so much I haven't got. And the prices.

It is obviously with me for life, a drug I can't give up, and one

I don't even want to give up. I want to know more and have more. I dare not tell you what I've spent in the last two years. If my wife ever finds out . . . I just can't understand why Gibbons' profits are down. They've had a fortune out of me. And are they grateful? Are they heckers.

Stamps is an individual hobby. Or should it be stamps are an individual hobby? Anyway, you do it on your own and that's one of the things I like about it. You don't have to ring someone up or book a court. But there's a difference between being alone, which is nice, and being lonely.

I'm now quite used to everyone else in this house thinking I've gone potty, refusing to look at my latest capture, putting their fingers in their ears when I tell them something really amazing about this Penny Red with a Maltese Cross and, listen to this, there's a number inside it which looks like, yes it does, really, it must be, a number 4, the one I've been looking for all these months. I can quite understand their lack of interest. It is my hobby, after all.

It's the big wide professional stamp world which depresses me. I feel somehow excluded from it. All those acres and acres of words and adverts in the stamp mags about things I don't know anything about, written in what reads like a foreign language. It all seems like a conspiracy. Have I been completely taken for a ride, collecting these silly bits of paper? All they appear to want is my money. Then they can go off and talk amongst themselves. I plan to talk to myself. You are invited to listen.

I used to hate stamp shops. During the first year that I became a collector, I always felt so miserable and depressed every time I came out of one. Not because I couldn't afford all the goodies they had. Not because it let me see all the stuff I didn't know existed, so how could I ever complete my puny little collection. No, the main reason I hated going into stamp shops was that they always seemed such horrid people.

Now I love stamp shops. In every new town I always search

them out, making huge detours, telling my children there's an interesting old house down here, or let's find a good caff, dragging them unwillingly along. When I'm on the scent of a new stamp shop, I'm very hard to stop.

They groan and scream and shout when eventually we've ended up outside this faded, shabby little shop, and immediately stamp their little feet and refuse to go any further. So we split. I send them off with money for ice cream, telling them to come back in three hours, or three days if they like. I'll still be here.

There's always the chance that in a new shop they might just have what you want, that elusive last MX with the number

"He says he is interested in anything to do with UFO's or outer space on stamps."

inside, or the plate you've never tracked down, or the last in the set. And you never know, they might all be half-wits, not knowing the true price of such stamps. You know the prices, cos you've been searching for months. Some chance. But we all live in hope.

The trouble was that during my first year as a paid-up Stamp Bug, I was collecting railway stamps. Thematic collectors, as we all know, are a despised race. I just had to go into a shop and

14

say eh, scuse me, your worship, your majesty, cough, cough, to be completely ignored.

Stamp shop owners are always bending over in a far corner, tweezing away, looking terribly busy and self-important. They don't really want to be disturbed, least of all by some fool wanting to buy something. As a generalisation, I would say that stamp shop owners, give or take a few exceptions, and of course I don't mean any of my friends, tut tut, what a suggestion, don't like people.

They're almost as bad as publicans. Deep down, every Mine Host wants everyone chucked out of his pub, this minute, and never allowed in again. Stamp dealers don't actively hate the human race. That takes up too much energy. They just wish we'd all quietly go away without silly questions and infantile requests.

Most of all, they don't like thematic collectors, though I think this is improving slightly. 'Got any railway stamps' is a pretty dopey thing to ask them. I know that. You feel like a kid. It's no use showing off your knowledge, asking for an 1869 three-cents USA blue. They just don't care. There's no money in railway stamps. They wave at some bundle of rubbish in the corner, beneath an illiterate hand-written sign which says any of these rubbish stamps for 5p each, now shut up and don't disturb me any more.

I once had a terrible row in a stamp shop in the Lake District. I was on to collecting *real* stamps by then, and wanting some GB QV, which I could see displayed, but none of his stamps had any prices on. I said how much are they and he said which one do you want? I said no, what are the prices? He said which one do you want?

Now I know this may seem peculiar to stamp dealers, but I enjoy casting my eye down endless displays of stamps, even ones I don't collect, just to see the prices. As far as he was concerned, it was a hanging offence, daring to suggest he should have priced all his boring stamps. I walked out in the end.

Stamp collectors lick 'em, stick 'em and mount 'em.

So many stamp shop people are so short-sighted. If they don't treat beginners like me nicely, or even worse, if they're not kind and helpful and considerate to schoolboys, where are their customers in the future going to come from?

On the whole, stamp shops are a disgrace, ill-arranged, scruffy and confused, with no attempt at displaying bargains or new excitements or even putting the same countries in the same corner. We serious collectors don't mind, do we? We're used to their funny ways. I just feel sorry for any stranger who stumbles into a stamp shop. They must never ever get impulse buyers. The object seems to be to repel outsiders and stop all impulses.

We collectors, once we get to know a shop, enjoy the lack of display, the lack of any movement or attempt to bring in the punters. It means that when there *is* the slightest little change, when a new cover has been pinned up, a new set arrived, or even a bit of dusting done, we regulars can spot it immediately.

And now, I come to the big exception. During the year I was depressed by all stamp shops, I had somehow missed the stamp shop which happens to be nearest to me. It means a walk across Hampstead Heath, as I live on the wrong side, and for some reason I'd never noticed it, tucked away down Flask Walk.

You won't believe this, but the first time I wandered in, hanging about, trying to look as if I knew what I was doing, smiling at prices, as if amused by their descriptions, the man behind the counter offered me a glass of sherry. I knew you would be amazed. He didn't know me. I hadn't spent a penny. You could have knocked me down with a packet of hinges.

They're called Eddie and Margaret, the couple who run the Hampstead Stamp Shop, and now, naturally enough, I'm a regular. I don't spend a great deal, but I drink a lot. I make a call every week, which is a social call, as much as anything. I've learned so much from them. They have time to explain things, just as long as you are willing to listen to things being explained. I've watched them with schoolboys on a Saturday morning, long before I knew them properly, and they take such pains and are so kind, often advising them not to buy certain new issues. End of commercial.

The motto then, for all amateur collectors, is do not despair. Expect most stamp shop owners not to be interested in you, then you won't be upset. They have better things to do. But persevere. One of these days you might meet one who's a member of the human race. And he might even offer you a drink.

UN COIN DE LA BOURSE AUX TIMBRES (CARRÉ MARIGNY)

One of my problems, doctor, is what to do with my stamps. Oh, I know you can just stick them up your album, which is Flora's favourite joke, probably everyone her age's favourite joke, but it's such a furtive thing, hiding away one's treasures in one's stamp albums, out of sight. It makes me feel like a Closet Collector.

When I came back to stamps, and became a born-again

stamp collector, I was delighted by all the technological advances that had been made while I'd been away. You just had hinges, when I was a lad, but even then I often used paste. Sometimes I just licked the backs, if they were mint, and stuck them in. I now know this is a hanging offence.

Plastic had arrived and taken over and I bought all those smart new style albums, at vast expense, with the plastic pockets all ready to have the pound notes, I mean the stamps, shoved in them. Then I discovered Hawid mounts and now what fun I have, cutting them up, measuring the sizes, putting them in the little frames which make even the crummiest stamp seem v. fine, perhaps average good, even superb on occasion, as they hide the thins and disguise the perfs.

All the same, and notwithsticking, you end up with albums, closed to the world, unseen by human eye. That is how my wife and family would prefer them to remain. They certainly don't want to see my boring stamps, thank you very much.

I don't have any stamp-collecting friends, sob sob, and I often feel very alone in this wicked philatelic world, so my albums remain stashed away, a pleasure only to themselves. But I *want* them to be seen. I am determined to Come Out as a stamp collector. I am not ashamed. Why should the Gay Libbers have all the fun?

What I have just done is to go out and buy fifty really beautiful frames. I bought one or two first of all in Habitat, at some expense, then discovered you can get a discount for a large order and they're a bargain. They're called Klipframes, and you can put them together in seconds, without losing any fingers. The small ones, 5 by 7 inches, work out about 70p each while the bigger ones, A4 size, are £1.25. Trific value, don't you think. Course, there's a rotten old VAT as well. (Get price list from Frame Up, Wembley HA9, Middlesex. I have no connection with them, never met them and no, my mother does not work there. End of unsolicited testimonial.)

Slowly and stealthily, I have been putting together one or two carefully chosen arrangements. You should see my

---

Stamp collectors do it with their tongues.

"I don't care if Hunter Davies has framed collections in every room of his house — enough is enough!"

collection of all the GB Royal commemoratives, from 1935 to Lady Di, which, as you well know is our eleventh Royal issue. The frame sets them off so well.

I've added the minimum of detail underneath. I refuse to go in for all that poncy handwriting and technical guff you see in those prize-winning stamp exhibitions. Who needs it?

I then hung a few of my collections in various parts of the house, on the dining-room wall, in the sitting room, very pleased with myself. I should have done it months ago. Not only have I created little works of art, good enough to decorate any wall, I will be bringing in new enthusiasts. All these teenage hooligans who pass through this house, on the way to the fridge to steal my beer, might stop a while and think, heh, her old man is on to something. Perhaps I should stop Hemeling and start collecting.

I came down in the morning and they'd all gone. The word couldn't have got round already. I know burglars are pretty smart round here. That 1948 Royal Silver Wedding £1 stamp was pretty expensive (cost me £24, but in v. nice condition). All the same, no one would break in just to steal that.

I discovered them back in my room, on the shelf with my stamp albums. My wife refuses to have them on her best walls. No taste at all. What a Philistine.

However, we struck a compromise. I can have them in the bathroom and in the lavatories. We have three lavatories in our house, which at long last has turned out a great bonus. I have almost filled my fifty frames with my clever little stamp arrangements and now have them crammed on every available lavatorial space.

Our lavs do get a lot of traffic, so I hope eventually that I will be helping the stamp industry. I intend to keep moving them around, to surprise people. When they think they're alone, my collection of Penny Reds will suddenly stare at them from over the cistern.

I might even get an award from the British Philatelic Federation. Services to stamps. Well, you're not serving anyone are you, sticking them away in a dark and gloomy album. I've come out of the closet. Into the closet.

Pete, Mary and John are heavily into triangulars...'

I 've not been collecting stamps for very long, but sometimes I look around my room and I think I've gone mad. Behind my back, they've all been breeding. Like amoeba, they've been dividing themselves up. I leave the room and they start a new section. Something is always happening. They've taken over my life and are now completely out of control. Help.

When people ask me what I collect, as of course they do all the time, the postman, the butcher, the baker, the VAT man, I say oh, not much really, just railway stamps and GB Victorian stamps. That used to be true, about a year ago. It still is, but those two broad areas have somehow split and spawned themselves into about twenty different collections.

Do you find this happens to you? You start off on one track then you disappear down your own exhaust, come out at a *cul de sac*, leave a little pile here, another bundle there, mixing the metaphors as you hare off on another wild-goose chase.

These twenty or so collections are now all over the house. About half of them are framed and adorning the lavatories. Others are in albums. The rest are in scruffy envelopes and packets, waiting to be arranged, waiting for me to get myself together and then get them together. If only I can remember why I bought them and what I'm going to do with them.

At the latest count, and in no particular order of merit or value, here are five of my current collections:

1) *HD on Stamps*. Yes, a little ego trip this one. I have so far got fourteen different Victorian stamps with my initials on, including three Penny Blacks and a very nice 1883 2s 6d. This collection could run and run, but is proving expensive. What is the point anyway? Who else would ever want my HD stamps? Horace Driver, Harry Dabbs, Hubert Dark, Humphry Davy, Hilary Dumpling, Humpty Dumpty — where are you and have you got any swaps?

2) *My Family on Covers*. I'm bored with this one already but they're in a huge frame and if I take them off the wall there will be a dirty mark. What I've done is collect Penny Reds on covers

---

Stamp collectors lick 'em all.

The top ten British stamps

(Approximate values, 1983 — supplied by Stanley Gibbons)

1	1902–4 King Edward VII 6d, dull purple, Inland Revenue overprint	£50,000 unused £30,000 used
2	1864–79 Queen Victoria 1d, plate 77	£35,000 unused £18,000 used
3	1882 Queen Victoria £1, brown-lilac, (watermark large anchor)	£25,000 unused £1,900 used
4	1902–4 King Edward VII 1/-, green and red, Board of Education overprint.	£23,000 unused £10,000 used
5	1885 Queen Victoria £1, brown-lilac, Inland Revenue overprint (watermark three crowns) with broken frame	£20,000 unused £3,500 used
6	1878 Queen Victoria £1, brown-lilac, (watermark Maltese Cross)	£20,000 unused £1,100 used
7	1883 Queen Victoria 10/-, grey (watermark large anchor)	£18,000 unused £950
8	1902 King Edward VII 10/- blue, Inland Revenue overprint	£17,000 unused £9,500 used
9	1890 Queen Victoria £1, brown-lilac, Inland Revenue overprint (watermark orbs) with broken frame	£17,000 unused £3,000 used
10	1878 Queen Victoria 10/- grey (watermark Maltese Cross)	£16,000 unused £800 used
	1902 King Edward VII £1, green, Inland Revenue overprint	£15,000 unused £3,250 used

which contain the initials of my wife and children — MD, CD, JD, FD. Wasn't I lucky that I didn't christen any of them Xandra, Yolande and Zebedee?

3) *George Stephenson and Rocket on stamps.* You'd be surprised how many times George has appeared on the stamps of foreign countries. Well, about six. I started this collection during the Liverpool-Manchester celebrations in 1981, but haven't done much on it recently. One of these days, if I'm spared, I'll arrange all the other bits of Rocket stuff I've got and make a nice display. One of these days.

4) *Royal Commemoratives.* I did this for Lady Di, ah, and have laid her out with all the ten previous Royal commemoratives, starting with the 1935 Silver Jubilee. Looks pretty good I think. I only collect the GB ones. I'm not daft. I've got enough rubbish as it is.

5) *Same Values.* Well, I know what I mean by this. In one frame, I have examples of all the penny stamps ever produced in GB, from 1840 to today. Naturally, I haven't gone in for the different plates, as my frame wouldn't be big enough, but I have managed to show the fourteen different designs of the penny stamp since it was first issued.

It's interesting to look back down the reigns and see how the penny stamp changed. And then how the old design came back. Very popular with visitors.

I've also done the same with the tuppenny stamps and the one-shilling stamps, now of course deceased. I'd really like to collect all the £1 stamps ever produced. But wouldn't we all.

Happy birthday, Stanley. Who would have thought when you began selling stamps in a corner of your father's chemist shop in Plymouth in 1856 that you would grow to be such a big boy? Not only is Stanley Gibbons, by appointment to HM the Queen, the biggest stamp dealer in the world, your present premises in London are also world renowned. Like the rest of Britain's two-million collectors, my page three fantasy is of being let loose at number 391 Strand. *Erotica philatelica.*

Perhaps your greatest gift to the world is your *Stamps of the World* catalogue which first appeared in 1865. It now comes out annually, with around two thousand pages, price £14.95, and it lists and prices every known stamp in the world. I can't think of any other hobby in which everything you could possibly ever buy is not only listed but given its own individual number. Every stamp collector in Britain and the Commonwealth, and in many other countries, uses the SG numbering. We would all be lost without it. Thanks, Stan.

I bought this catalogue when I first became a serious collector, and I found it totally confusing. It sells about 100,000 copies a year. If reference books were allowed on the *The Sunday Times* best-seller list, it would hammer almost every other book in sight.

One of its miniature versions, *Collect British Stamps*, which is a little paperback (it costs around £1.50) has sold 2,500,000 since it first appeared in 1967. Well done, Stanley.

It may seem churlish on such a happy occasion to start moaning, but you must admit, Stan, that the prices in your catalogues are the biggest single source of complaints from all beginners in the philatelic field.

I don't get too worried when I see those articles in the newspapers about some reporter trailing round three experts with the same stamp and getting three completely different offers. It happens in every hobby, every art form. There's probably some hack standing at the front counter of Sotheby's this minute with an Old Master, about to snigger to himself when they value it at half the price which Christies have already put on it. Oh, what fun, catching out the experts.

Personally, I'm a great disbeliever in experts. They are there to be used, and abused, but in the end you have to make your decisions. Anyone who sells something to or through the first dealer he goes to needs his head felt.

Such stories look worse when it comes to stamps because old SG, look there it is, in black and white in the catalogue, has put an exact price on every stamp. Here again I don't get too worried. A dealer makes you an offer based on what he thinks he can get for it. If he hasn't a customer in mind, or already has too many of those rotten stamps, or has no intention of going into that boring field, or knows little about that stamp anyway, he will make you an offer on what it is worth to *him*. So, you have to find him who will offer more.

Most days, someone goes into Gibbons in the Strand and says look here, Mr Gibbons, as one must be polite, according to your catalogue, this album which my great uncle has just left

"Who is this Stanley we keep hearing about?"

me is worth £600. I've gone through every stamp, found its number and that's the price *you've* put on them. Yet, the most I've been offered is £30. It's all a con, this stamp world, if you ask me, Mr Gibbons.

I put this specific question to them recently, based on a real example, and one of their experts slowly went through the explanation. The album had been built up by a boy in the 1950s, buying hundreds of stamps priced then at 1d each. It is true such stamps are now priced by them at 5p, but, alas, that is their selling price. They have thousands of such stamps and to them, each is worth virtually nothing. In fact the 5p is really a handling charge. So, sorry, £30 is all they would offer for the collection.

When it comes to older, rarer, apparently more expensive

stamps, the beginner can be equally disappointed, which is what happened to me when I bought a Penny Black for £25 and rushed to Gibbons who said it was worth £5. Yet there in their catalogue it says a used Penny Black, £150.

Now I know a dealer has to make a profit. They're all just shopkeepers after all. You expect them to add thirty per cent or so on to the price they paid, but — gee whiz — £5 for an item they are selling at £150. Silly old me. I didn't understand the system.

My little stamp was a load of rubbish. When they say £150

The Wit and Wisdom of Stamp Dealers

'Have you heard? I got paid by one of my customers.'
David Somerset

'Stamp collectors do it for fun. Stamp dealers do it for nothing.'

A. N. Lindsey-Bullock

---

for a Used Penny Black in their catalogue they mean one in 'fine average condition'. This is the phrase they use in the Introduction to *Collect British Stamps*. Even though now, two years later, I know how to read their catalogue, I maintain this wording is completely useless for the beginner.

'Fine' and 'average' appear to be easy words to understand, and the beginner thinks he knows what they mean, but Stanley Gibbons have their own interpretation.

'A stamp in fine, average condition', so one of their experts told me, 'is one without faults, creases, pin holes, or surface damage and has four margins and full perforations.' It is a pity they don't say all that, and more, perhaps with diagrams, in *Collect British Stamps*.

It would appear, in other words, that when you read an SG price, you are looking at the price for the very best examples of that particular stamp, perhaps the top ten per cent which exist.

Stamp collectors do it with Gibbons.

That's really not much use to the beginner. I would like to know the median price, the average price for the *average* stamp, not the top end of the market.

My friendly SG expert denied that their prices only refer to a small minority, and says they refer to stamps which 'collectors aim for'.

From my few years' experience, reading scores of auction lists, of estimates and prices realised, I would say that the present average price for a good used Penny Black, which has none of the faults listed above, is around £60. Surely that would be a more meaningful price to put in their catalogue than £150?

For example, I have in front of me details of an SG Auction in which they have several pages of used Penny Blacks. While one or two examples, in the rarer plates, are estimated at £200, there are many described as having good margins and in fine condition priced at only £50.

Estimates are usually on the low side, to bring in the punters, which is why I maintain the average selling price is therefore around £60.

One of the major problems with the SG catalogue prices being so high is that all over the country, local dealers are tempting in the unsuspecting by offering bargains at, say, £10 when the official *Catalogue Price* is £100. They always give you both prices, to show how generous they are, and they can bring out the bible to prove their assertions. In almost every case, this reference to the Catalogue price means very little. They are not comparing like with like.

So, two points then to remember if you are not quite familiar with the SG Catalogues. It is *their* selling price, what they will charge you for that particular stamp. The fact that this catalogue price is now bandied about by dealers throughout the world, as if it relates to all such stamps, is not the fault of Gibbons.

Secondly, those prices refer to the *best* examples. Most of us haven't got the best examples and probably never will, though Gibbons will be glad to sell them to you.

However, we should be grateful that such a catalogue exists, which is comprehensive and is accepted by everyone, even if it takes practice to use it. We should be lost without it. Thank you, Stanley.

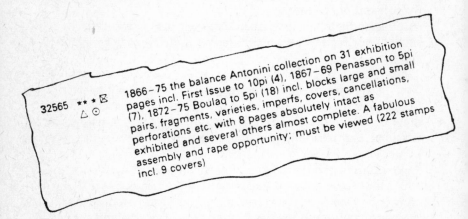

32565 ** * ⊠
△ ⊙

1866–75 the balance Antonini collection on 31 exhibition pages incl. First Issue to 10pi (4), 1867–69 Penasson to 5pi (7), 1872–75 Boulaq to 5pi (18) incl. blocks large and small pairs, fragments, varieties, imperfs, covers, cancellations, perforations etc. with 8 pages absolutely intact as exhibited and several others almost complete. A fabulous assembly and rape opportunity; must be viewed (222 stamps incl. 9 covers)

From David Feldman's auction catalogue, April 10, 1983, offering a lot of Egyptian stamps. Let's hope there are no Mummies amongst them . . .

I was in my local stamp shop, frittering away my money, frittering away my life, when a man at the counter asked if they had any Cape triangulars. I edged myself closer, being nosey, though of course I'm not interested in such fripperies. How can I be? I've got my railway stamps and my GB Victorian stamps to keep me going for this lifetime.

When I come back in my next re-incarnation, (and I've got my name down to be Stanley Gibbons on my return), I might then have time and space and cash and inclination for such diversions.

'Got anything new in my line?' I asked my friendly stamp lady who said: 'No, but you can have a glass of sherry if you like.' 'I'm still looking for the 1867 £5 orange,' I said, as I do every week. I know they can cost £10,000 and I haven't got that amount right now, but I keep on hoping she'll dig up one for about £15. Well, one can hope. There must be some rubbish examples somewhere that nobody wants. It will then almost complete my collection of rubbish Victorian stamps. Sorry, space fillers. That makes them sound not too bad.

The gentleman next to me had a South African accent so I thought he must know what he's doing, I'll edge even nearer. She had no Cape triangulars but she showed him a 1926 South African triangular which looked rather attractive, especially the price, 75p. That's the sort of stamp I really like to collect.

He didn't buy anything but when he'd left the shop, I moved along the counter and had a look at the stuff he'd refused. In a mad rush of impulse buying, I bought the SA triangular for 70p. (The rush to the head hadn't quite relieved me of all my senses and I managed to get discount, being a regular customer and all that.)

As I left the shop, I told her to keep a look out for a *real* Cape triangular, one of the original ones of 1853. I might be interested. Not promising. You never know.

Every keen stamp collector should have a Cape triangular, just as every keen collector should have a Penny Black. No need to get good ones. There are some things one collects for sentimental reasons. Bad examples can be just as interesting as good examples.

Did you know that it was the Cape triangulars which put Stanley Gibbons on the map? Made his fortune for him in fact. One day in 1863 two sailors came into the little chemist's shop in Plymouth, owned by Stanley's father, and said they had a bag of stamps which they'd won in a raffle during shore leave in Cape Town. That was their story anyway.

Young Stanley had been given a counter in his father's shop, and was trying to set himself up as a stamp dealer, so he said, quick as a flash, I'll give you £5 for the sack full. The sailors were very pleased, thinking we've got a right dumdum here, imagine anyone wanting to buy old stamps. Young Stanley went on to sell the sackful of stamps, all Cape triangulars, and made himself a profit of £500. Nice one Stanley.

So you see, for historic reasons, not just philatelic, one

Italy produced the world's first official airmail stamp — the 25-cent in 1917.

Italy produced the only issue of 3D stamps — the UN commemorative stamps, 1956.

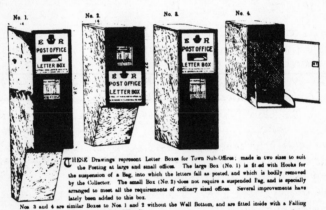

THESE Drawings represent Letter Boxes for Town Sub-Offices; made in two sizes to suit the Posting at large and small offices. The large Box (No. 1) is fitted with Hooks for the suspension of a Bag, into which the letters fall as posted, and which is bodily removed by the Collector. The small Box (No. 2) does not require a suspended Bag, and is specially arranged to meet all the requirements of ordinary sized offices. Several improvements have lately been added to this box.

Nos. 3 and 4 are similar Boxes to Nos. 1 and 2 without the Wall Bottom, and are fitted inside with a Falling Flap and Wirework, similar to the Cast Iron Pillar Boxes.

The advantages of these Boxes are numerous in the saving of time, trouble, and responsibility. The Box, being made to open from the outside, is cleared by the Collector in the same way as Street Pillar and Wall Boxes, thus enabling Sunday and early morning collections to be made, which cannot be done at Town Sub-offices fitted with the ordinary Letter Boxes.

These Boxes are made of strong well-seasoned Wood, dove-tailed together; the Door and Front exposed to Street is plated with Thick Sheet Steel, and is fitted with a moveable Escutcheon. *(The Lock and Keys, and an Enamelled Plate showing the Hours of Collection, are provided by the Department.)* The Plate is fitted in a groove from the top of the door; and the Tablet Frame is fixed at the right-hand upper corner, as shown in drawings, so that the tablet can be readily changed. The exposed Face of the Box is painted in Vermilion, and the Box Body stained Mahogany. *If the Locks which are supplied by the Department are sent with the order, they will be fitted on without extra charge.* Thousands of these Boxes are now in use throughout the country; have stood the test for upwards of 20 years, and given perfect satisfaction.

PRICE OF LARGE BOXES, Nos. 1 and 3, including large Enamelled Aperture Plate, *without Lock* ... £2 10 0 *Nett.*
PRICE OF SMALL BOXES, Nos. 2 and 4, including large Enamelled Plate, *without Lock* ... ... £2 2 0 *Nett.*

Packing Case Free.   Exclusive of Carriage or Fixing.

In ordering the Collection and Indicator Tablets for the above Boxes, please order Size F.1.

should have a Cape triangular. That's what I told myself as I walked home. I then looked up *Stamps of the World* on my return and found that the 1861 penny red triangular can cost £10,000. Bloody hell. What have I done?

In the meantime, I am working on a collection of cheap triangulars. I've just got a nice set from Hungary of triangular dogs for only 30p and some Russian triangular cars at 50p. Oh, and I've got two nice ones from New Zealand, showing the Queen as a triangular Princess. They cost only a few triangular pennies.

Here we go again. Another collection getting started, as if I haven't got enough. I must be mad. What on earth am I going to do with them? Does Mr Hawid do triangular mounts? More problems.

Stick to stamps.

Here is a little stamp conundrum so concentrate very hard. Okay, I know you need all your wits and your best specs for really good articles written by real stamp experts, and of course for all the Bargain Buy advertisements in very very small print where you just have to blink once and you've confused the UM Mint column with the VF Used column. All the same, here is my smart question:

Why can I give a Penny Red as a personal present to Neil Kinnock but not to Margaret Thatcher?

That's got you. No, it's not political. For the same reason I can't find one for Willie Whitelaw but I've got one here I can give to Roy Jenkins. (If of course he was called Woy Jenkins, then I couldn't possibly give him one.)

Give up? Oh, you already guessed. I'd forgotten how clever you were. I suppose you must be, though. To have got this far.

Penny Reds, like Penny Blacks and Tuppenny Blues and some of the other early Victorian GB stamps, all have letters in the corner of each stamp. When I first noticed this, I presumed that you could find all the letters of the alphabet, if you went

"He says he would like to see one of your Penny Reds!"

through enough stamps, but, ah ha, the letters only run so far through the alphabet.

The point of putting different letters on each stamp was as a security measure. It was thought the counterfeiters would have a more difficult time.

They produced 240 differently lettered penny stamps in a sheet, because in those far-off lovely days, we hadn't gone decimal and there were 240 pennies in a pound. Down one side they ran the first twenty letters of the alphabet, from A–T, and across they used the first 12 letters, A–L. Are you still there? Or are you already putting pen to typewriter to tell me I'm a dum-dum and I've got the explanation all wrong.

Anyways, the result is that you can find stamps with people's initials on, as long as their Christian name begins with a letter between A and T and their surname between A and L.

I collect Penny Reds according to their letters. I file them away carefully and when I go to see people, especially rich and famous and successful people (oh, I know lots of those), I make them a present of their own personalised Penny Red stamp. *They are amazed.* I promise you.

I recently gave one to Lew Grade. He is someone who has had most of the good things in life, cigars as big as a tube train, a salary as big as a phone number, but I was able to say to him, close your eyes Lew, I am going to give you a present you have never had in your whole life before. Believe me.

He was politely grateful, but I could see he was rather bemused by this little scrap of paper, even though I had framed it so beautifully, in one of my famous frames. Then I pointed out the initials of the stamp — LG. Wow. He was dee-lighted.

I found one with the initials HE and gave it to Harold Evans. How do you think I became Philatelic Correspondent of *The Sunday Times*?

The point about these little personal gifts, apart from the bribery and corruption angle, is that non-stamp people are not only thrilled to see their initials, they think this is a very *valuable* gift.

They have in their little minds that Penny Red must be something like a Penny Black and they think, wrongly, it's terribly expensive. I just mutter something incoherent, no no, it was nothing, really, just a little something, thought you'd like it, did take me quite a while to find that particular one, but no, it wasn't *very* expensive . . .

You and I, being stamp lovers, know that a 1841 Penny Red costs about £1 and as for the 1858 perforated Penny Reds, they're looked upon by most dealers as rubbish stamps and you can get them for 30p. But, please, don't tell Lord Grade or Mr Evans these prices, next time you meet them. We stamp collectors should maintain a little mystery in our lives.

POST OFFICE JUBILEE

UNIFORM PENNY POSTAGE

AT SOUTH KENSINGTON MUSEUM, 2ND JULY 1890.

THE NORTH MAIL MAKING FOR HIGHGATE 1793 AT 8 MILES AN HOUR

Top Ten World Stamps, 1983

(Approximate values according to Stanley Gibbons)

1 British Guiana 1
   cent black on
   magenta of 1856   (S.G.23)   £425,000 unused

2 Mauritius 'Post
   Office' 1d red of
   1847   (S.G.1)   £375,000 unused
                                          £140,000 used

3 Mauritius 'Post
   Office' 2d blue of
   1847   (S.G.2)   £240,000 unused
                                          £140,000 used

4 Bermuda red 'Penny
   Perot' 1848–61   (S.G.04)   £100,000 used

5 Hawaii 2 cents blue
   of 1851   (S.G.1)   £60,000 unused
                                          £30,000 used

6 British Guiana 2
   cents rose 'Cotton
   Reel' 1851   (S.G.1)   £55,000 used

7 Great Britain 1902
   6d purple 'IR'
   OFFICIAL'   (S.G.023)   £50,000 unused
                                          £30,000 used

8 Ceylon 4d dull rose
   of 1857   (S.G.9)   £50,000 unused
                                          £4,500 used

9	Canada 12d black of 1851	(S.G.4)	£42,000 unused £38,000 used
10	Great Britain 1864–79 Queen Victoria 1d red plate 77		£35,000 unused £18,000 used

Countries most collected by stamp collectors living in Britain

1	Great Britain	6	Hong Kong
2	New Zealand	7	Falkland Island
3	Australia	8	Vatican
4	Canada	9	Israel
5	USA	10	Ireland

Most popular themes with UK postcard collectors

1	Typographical	6	Military
2	Glamour	7	Political
3	Artists	8	Royalty
4	Advertising	9	Ships
5	Humour	10	Costumes

FIG. L.—Spring-back Binder for Loose-leaf Album ("Paragon," etc.).

US top twenty themes

The most popular theme in the United States is Animals, followed by Medical Subjects and Space. These rankings are from a tabulation of the collecting interest of members of the American Topical Association. But the most popular themes over the past twenty years are (1) Animals, (2) Space, and (3) Ships.

Rank 1982	Topic	Rank 1978	Ranking 20 Year Average
1	Animals	3	1
2	Medical Subjects	4	6
3	Space	1	2
4	Ships	2	3
5	Americana	5	9
6	Music	7	13
7	Religion	12	12
8	Railroads	6	8
9	Flowers	9	4
10	Sports	8	7
11	Art	11	5
12	Birds	10	10
13	Marine Life	17	*
14	United Nations	18	14
15	Insects	15	20
16	Aviation	*	*
17	Scouts	13	11
18	Europa	*	18
19	Stamps on Stamps	14	17
20	Masonry	*	16

* = Ranking not in Top 20

You need three for a strip.

Stamp collectors soak 'em off.

I am always being asked questions about stamps. Oh, we experts like to help lesser mortals, pass on our great knowledge and long experience of dealing with the really tricky problems that crop up from time to time. You know, things like which selfish person in this house has just used the last stamp because I want it to send off my entry in the Kellogg's Corn Flake competition.

The really hard question is how should I sell my stamps? I know it's hard because I'm always asking it myself. Go away, Hunt, I usually say, and stop asking such silly questions, but now and again I listen to my own advice.

There are two main ways of selling stamps — either to a dealer or through an auction. If you're sitting comfortably, I'll tell you my experiences. Pull up a hinge and sit down. Feel free to use my tweezers.

My local stamp dealer in Hampstead, to whom I am devoted, sent me a catalogue which says on it: 'We are constantly in need of good single items and collections to replenish stock.' I rushed to my swop albums, dug out my spares, all those sets I was forced to buy when I only wanted one, all those Penny Reds I got cheap, thinking I didn't have them, then discovered my album was already full of them. I put all this rubbish, I mean these good single items, in a carrier bag, and rushed over to the shop.

She was very nice about it. She did smile. They're in a cash flow situation, see, like every stamp shop in the universe. What they don't want is stamps, thank you very much, not at the moment, and especially not those. They want to *sell* not buy.

Over the last year I've probably asked about a dozen stamp shops in various places if they would like to buy any of my stamps, and I've got the bum's rush from them all. I point out that in their windows and in their advertisements, they are always boasting that they will PAY CASH, STAMPS WANTED, BEST PRICES, HURRY HURRY HURRY. Now I know this is a simple ruse to get us punters in.

So when you ask me about selling to dealers, I have to say next question please.

Which brings me to auctions and so saying I set off for Bond Street to see Mr Sotheby. Well, one might as well start at the top, at the world's number one auction house. I carefully got together some of my *better* pieces. I know I'm always going on about my Penny Reds, but I do have some good ones, with a great variety of Maltese Crosses and Town Numbers, and Numbers inside Maltese Crosses. See, I knew you'd be interested.

"Which signals would you prefer to have ignored sir? Your ear has just outbid your toe!"

The gentleman at Sotheby's seemed quite impressed. I mean, he didn't throw them back at me, or snigger to himself, or discover a previous engagement. Hmm, about £20 worth here, he said. Thank you. He handed them back to me. Turns out that Sotheby's don't handle lots under £100. Nobody told me that. I hadn't noticed it in any of their catalogues. All that way to Bond Street for nothing.

So friends, I think that answers all the questions for today. To sum up, when next you ask yourself how do I sell my stamps, the answer is you must be joking. Your place in life, as an ordinary collector, is to *buy* stamps. Please remember that.

Professor Emmanuel Herrmann of Austria created the world's first postcard in 1869.

The world's first postal datestamp was created in London in 1661 by Henry Bishop, the Postmaster General. It was his answer to criticisms that letters were being delayed in the post.

I have been criticised from time to time for giving publicity to my local stamp shop, going on about how wonderful they were, compared with some grumpy old stamp dealers I could name but didn't, how they were so kind to young people and children, helped old philatelists across the road, always patted thematic collectors on the head and kissed baby stamp bugs in their prams. I also happened to admit that they often gave me a glass of sherry, when I chanced to stray into their emporium. That was what really had the nation's stamp dealers going mad.

Well, anyway. Guess what's happened.

I went in last week, hanging about, poking through the special offers, examining the curling covers, turning over the plastic bumper bundles, as if I hadn't seen any of them before which I have done, all summer, and I asked if there was anything new in my line.

I don't know why I've picked up this elliptical conversation. Am I ashamed to come straight out and say excuse me, have you any new Queen Victoria material? It's as if I'm in Soho, asking for the hard stuff, you know, nudge nudge, the stuff you keep in the back room, say no more.

Yes, we have something new to sell, said Eddie, my friendly stamp dealer. The shop. Well, you could have knocked me down with one of those half pee Victorian stamps.

It was a long and sad story. They're right in the middle of Hampstead village, which of course is hard cheese, as the rates must be horrendous, but I'd always thought they weren't in too bad a financial position as they have got a ten-year lease. Turns out that despite having such a lease they still pay £100 a week in rent and rates. Then of course there's heating and all the other overheads. Just to cut even, without paying himself or his wife Margaret a salary, they have to sell £700 worth of stamps every week. This they failed to do all year. They've been running at a loss, living on their capital.

All small businesses are having a hard time. Nobody owes stamp dealers a living. It's not exactly war work. But they do provide an excellent service in a stamp-less area. I've seen the kids and families on Saturday mornings, having good times, enjoying themselves, learning the rudiments of a hobby which will give them pleasure through life.

I've often worried that perhaps they did stock too many fun stamps, the wallpaper issues which those dopey non-countries issue all the time, which we superior collectors wouldn't even let our servants keep in their albums. But I've *admired* them for doing so. There can't be much profit in them, but that's how most schoolchildren begin.

Eddie puts it all down to the recession, which is probably correct. If times were good and stable, yet their shop was still doing badly, they could perhaps deduce that their prices were too high or their personality didn't fit and try to do something about it. As it is, they can think of *nothing* to improve trade.

I suggested moving the stamps into the cellar and having a coffee bar upstairs. Or how about selling books in half the shop. Surely there must be some way of diversifying, till the economy improves. Dancing girls perhaps. Rubik cubes even.

No, they have now decided to try to sell their lease. So far, five people have approached them about turning their stamp shop into a boutique. Dear God. Hampstead is already a sea of boutiques. They've refused, so far. They would like it to remain a stamp shop, even if it means the sort of awful stamp shop where they put one expensive stamp in the window in a gold frame with a discreet spot light.

You might say, in your cynical way, that it serves them right. They should not have encouraged the kids on Saturday mornings, cluttering up their premises, and certainly not given free sherries to browsers like me. Ah well. A light will go out of my life.

They've provided a flesh and blood contact with the world of stamps these last two years. Through them, I've met other suckers, I mean collectors, and swapped stories and experiences. Where will I go now? There's not another stamp shop for miles. I rarely have the energy or the time to drag down to the Strand, wonderful though all those new places are.

I have had a weekly routine in which I've worked out a round walk, taking in the stamp shop. Now, I'll be all alone, just me and my albums, talking to the catalogues, ogling all the adverts in *Stamp & Postal History News*. They can save the whales. Why can't they save the Hampstead stamp shop . . .

Two Definitives

'Philatelists are people who collect little bits of paper that other people have licked.'
                              Sir Harold Nicolson (1886–1968)

'Stamp collectors are people who pay money to acquire stamps. Philatelists are collectors who borrow other people's stamps to study them.'
                    Raife Wellsted, Curator, National Postal Museum

I did not know I was taking part in one of the world's newest and fastest growing hobbies when last January I happened to be in Stanley Gibbons, poking about their stamp counters, when I went up the stairs and wandered into a department marked Bonds and Shares.

Inside the room, I came upon the most marvellously engraved pictures of railway trains, puffing away through sylvan landscapes, surrounded by highly decorated borders and copper-plate handwriting. For £3.50 I bought one of these beautiful engravings and found that I was the owner of a hundred £5 shares in something called the Gulf, Mobile and Ohio Railroad, a company which disappeared in 1940.

"That can't be classed as ephemera collecting, George!"

As a share certificate, it was worthless. As a nice picture of a railway train, to me it was a bargain. It is about 12in by 8in and I still have it framed above my desk. I worked out that it was about thirty times the size of any of the railway stamps in my collection, stamps which I collect because they have railway trains on them. You did not need a microscope to see the detail. It was a work of art in itself.

I went back later and lashed out £10 on a Rock Island Line share certificate which if anything was even prettier, and with musical as well as railway connections. What a bargain. I nearly rang Lonnie Donegan to tell him to come quick.

There can be few hobbies which can truthfully be said to be brand new but, according to all the experts, and there are now dozens of dealers in London, and regular auctions held at places like Sotheby's, the collecting of defunct bond and share certificates began as a serious occupation in Britain only in 1977. Almost overnight, bits of paper considered absolutely worthless were changing hands for hundreds, even thousands, of pounds.

I bought quite a few old railway bonds over the next few weeks, rarely paying more than £15 each, listening in awe as the experts told me that what I should really be buying were Chinese and Russian bonds. I didn't like the look of them, or the prices. I only liked pretty pictures of puffers.

I could hardly believe what they were saying about the Chinese government stuff, but they assured me, bringing out the facts and figures, that a Chinese government 5 per cent gold loan of 1908 which had cost £350 in May 1979 was now, in April 1980, just a year later, priced at £1,500. Even more astronomical, an 1898 Chinese bond went at auction for £15,000. It's still a world record.

Along with the fancy prices, they introduced a fancy name for the collecting of old bond and share certificates — scripophily. Very soon, several hardback books appeared, references for the mad rush of speculators who were now pouring into the new hobby, hoping that the prices would rise by another three hundred per cent in the next year, just as they had risen in some cases in the previous year.

Carried along with such excitement, I went really mad and paid £320 for an American Express 1856 certificate, signed by Mr Wells and Mr Fargo. I don't know anything about China or Russia or their funny-looking financial shares but I do know

---

Stamp collectors peel 'em off.

---

who Mr Wells and Mr Fargo were. I thought if I stick to what I like, and what I know about, which is railways, then to me they will always be valuable, regardless of what the dopey speculators are doing out there in the mad world of investment portfolios.

Today, I sit here rather smugly, knowing that the first boom in bonds and shares is over. Those Chinese and Russian things came tumbling. I see that one of those Chinese shares of 1898, which fetched £15,000 a year ago, is up for sale at Stanley Gibbons in New York on March 6, in their first auction of bonds in America. They estimate it will fetch, so they hope, around £10,000. I think they will be lucky.

An American Express share, just like mine, went for £420 at Sotheby's not long ago, but I do not suppose I could make much profit on all the other American railroad shares I now own, all bought very cheaply. However, I bought them for my amusement, not as an investment. At the same time, my little mind told me that there will always be rich Americans, willing to spend money to buy their history, whereas you do not come across many Russians and Chinese with money to burn.

Now that the mad, daft days are over, at least for the moment, and the speculators have retreated, the hobby will settle down and become quietly respectable, which is a much healthier situation all round. I stumbled into it for the railway history, and I have considerably enlarged my knowledge of American railway road companies, but the different printing and engraving techniques are equally fascinating, and far easier to appreciate than stamps.

For those in the City, or involved in financial matters, collecting old bonds of any sort is of great interest, living proof that money is never dead, even when it has died. The first great avalanche of stocks and share certificates came with the South Sea Bubble in 1720. From then until the early nineteenth century, it was mainly government stock which kept stock brokers busy. There was a brief period in the 1820s when it was all the rage to invest in South American stocks, but it was the arrival of railways from 1840 which started the real share boom.

You can follow the history of wars and famines, revolutions and expansions as various governments round the world have shoved out bonds for people to buy, most of them eventually worthless until the arrival of scripophily.

There is now a growing, though modest, market in old British industrial bonds, especially those with some historic significance. They tend not to be as ornate as the American, Russian or Chinese. I put in a bid recently at Sotheby's for a Liverpool–Manchester Railway certificate which they estimated might go for around £200, which sounded reasonable for such an historic railway. I closed my eyes and bid £210. It went for £420.

There must be thousands of lofts round the country with old stocks and share certificates lying rotting, with nobody aware of their new value. I wouldn't sell them, if I were you. This is not the time. Just get them out and dust them and if they look pretty, as most of them do, displaying the sort of printing expertise we will never see again, and if they relate to a company with interesting local or national connections, then if I were you, I'd frame them nicely. You could have money hanging on the wall.

The numbering of houses to help postmen began in Paris in 1463. The first area to be numbered was the Pont Notre Dame district.

The highest street number in Britain is 2679 Stratford Road, Hockley Heath, West Midlands. The highest in Scotland is 2629, London Road, Mount Vernon, Glasgow.

Thirteen-year-old P. J. Rixon of Shefford in Bedfordshire has kindly sent us his own amazing fact about the birth of stamps:

Did you know that 240 people entered the Treasury competition to design a stamp in 1839? By some incredible coincidence, all 240 designed the identical Black stamp, with Queen Victoria's head on it. The only difference was that each competitor put his initials in the bottom corner. The Post Office liked them so much that they fixed all the entries together in one sheet. All the stamps with HD on were designed by Head Dunce.

Not content with that world exclusive, Master Rixon has also given us an extract from a letter he says he has just discovered . . .

Dear Penny Black,
How I have miss-printed you. I must come and see-tenant you soon. I prefer though not to gum by aero-gramme. I like a solid flaw under my doctor bladeins. I went to Hospital in Harrow perforation the other die. The doctored stamp said I was invert good health but I have topenny Blue take it marginmarkingly. Myniature sheet Aunt who is blind perforation wrote to taille douce meter marks that she is die proofing to tell you about her new block overprint flawts in Zemstvos. I've got her letterpress at home so you'll have to coilect it one dayte. She sent a photogravure as well. I'll see yused some time.
Yours Sinsurchargely,
Stanley.

Stamp collectors soon become unhinged.

I was laughing so much this morning over my muesli that my wife said quick, quick, let me have a look, it must be very funny to make *you* laugh at breakfast time. I handed her a stamp catalogue which had come through the post from Embassy Philatelists, one of those duplicated sheets you must have seen, hand typed, which usually boasts in the first paragraph how terribly fortunate they have been to purchase a large accumulation at a very reasonable price and they can offer the following wonderful bargains, hurry hurry, while stocks last.

My wife looked at it briefly, turned over the smudgy pages, then threw it in the waste paper basket.

My post is enormous these days, ever since I became a serious stamp collector, which drives everyone mad except me. I probably get a stamp catalogue of some sort every day. I enjoy the glossy photographs, glossy paper and glossy sterile prose produced by Sotheby's, Phillips, Gibbons and Robson Lowe, and now and again I put in a ridiculously low bid, just to see what happens, but I get most pleasure out of reading the one-man operations. Behind these amateur sheets, produced from some back room in Carlisle or Bognor Regis, there are real, living breathing personalities, struggling to get across their wares, and their enthusiasms.

I think I must have bought something from Embassy once at Stampex and I've been on their mailing list ever since. It's always a highlight for me, when their latest ravings, I mean listings, arrive, so I carefully picked it out of the basket and retired to my room.

'Yet another bumper edition with over 1200 BARGAINS for your delectation. Indeed wise is the man who fills those gaps now whilst prices are still low before speculation and boom times send them hurtling upwards. Super buys at VALUE FOR MONEY prices...has to be a GIVEAWAY...If you see an expensive item you would like but cannot afford it immediately THEN DON'T CRY, we can help with instalment...'

After all that hard sell, my eyes slightly shell-shocked with the capital letters and underlining, I then worked my way through the individual items.

Barry Fitzgerald, for such is the name which signs all those exhortations, never uses one adjective if he can drag in two, or

"That's the last time I'll deliver a registered air mail from Transylvania!"

even three. 'Magnificent fine looker, lovely scarce shade, clear crisp strike, super cheap bargain.'

It takes time to understand his scale of superlatives. Some stamps are difficult, some very difficult and some exceedingly difficult. Others are excellent, super excellent and truly excellent. Colours are always lovely, fresh, beautiful or intense. He even distinguishes between stamps which are Underrated, Very Underrated and Ten Times Scarcer than Normal.

There are occasional typing mistakes, and words missed out, which makes the prose even harder to follow, especially as he throws in jokes when he can't think of any other way to fill up the lines. In this latest list for example, he is offering a 1872 6d which is 'tied onto small neat piece buy (Ha! Ha!) London duplex.' No wonder my wife failed to see what was so funny. You've got to be an expert on Embassy Speak to realise that Barry for once must have noticed he'd made a typing mistake, but had turned it into a joke, or what he thinks is a joke. I could do a PhD on philatelic prose.

Mr Fitzgerald now has a stall in the London International Stamp Centre in Covent Garden, according to his notepaper. So I happened to be going to town, so I popped in one afternoon, hoping to see the bold Barry in the flesh.

He is young and lean and as bouncy and as full of old chat as I had expected from his literature. I admired his enthusiasm, managing to admit that last year had been a very bad year for business, yet without moaning. Stamp dealers are as bad as farmers for moaning on, given half a chance. As if we poor collectors haven't got our own problems. However, I did buy some of his bargains, which were good value.

It takes him three whole days to type out his lists, so he says, which he does with one finger. When he first began back in 1975, he had only a hundred items to sell, so life and typing was easier. Now with twelve hundred items he collapses exhausted after each session.

He still tries to work in some jokes, if he has the energy. 'Did you see my last list? I was very fond of one remark in that one. It was a 1880 2½d, SG 157, plate 22, mint. You *must* remember it. I put "stain on Queen's bun (THIS IS NOT A SPELLING MISTAKE!)" '

Ho ho ho. Who says stamps aren't fun.

He said life was tough and he had to work much harder than he did three years ago. In those days, he was selling to a lot of investors who didn't care for stamps and were just financial machines. Now, he is selling purely to collectors, which he says is five times as hard but five times more enjoyable.

Stamp collectors stick to their hobby.

Prohibited Mail

Most countries in the world have a list of certain things they don't allow to be sent through the post from abroad. Many of the banned items are obviously to protect some vested interest at home, or to protect their citizens in some way, though very often the reasons are rather obscure, at least to outsiders. Here is a selection of prohibited mail throughout the world.

After all, you might be foolish enough to want to send natural manure to Poland, ladies' handbags to Afghanistan or foreign bank notes to Switzerland. *Switzerland?* Don't they like foreign currency in Switzerland? Nope. That is definitely not allowed.

Country	Prohibition
Afghanistan:	Ladies' handbags
Albania:	Dead animals
Algeria:	Matches
Argentina:	Twine
Bahrain:	Carbon paper
Bangladesh:	Rose-coloured quinine
Belgium:	Absinthe
Belize:	Daggers
Benin:	Gramophone records
Bhutan:	Antiques
Bolivia:	Cigarettes
Botswana:	Honey
Brazil:	Postage stamps
Bulgaria:	Used footwear
Canada:	Plumages
Chile:	Condensed milk
China:	Wrist watches

Colombia:	Cork
Cuba:	Maps
Cyprus:	Leeches
Denmark:	Cigarette papers
Ecuador:	Babyfeeders with tubes
Egypt:	Sticky substances usable for the capture of birds
Fiji:	Sword sticks
Finland:	Goods originating in Southern Rhodesia
France:	Funeral urns
Germany (DDR):	Duplicating machines
Germany (FR):	Parasites
Greece:	Playing cards
Guatemala:	Whistles as used by police
Guinea:	Babyfeeders with long tubes
Guyana:	Shaving-brushes made in Japan
Hungary:	Eggplant
Iceland:	Hay
India:	Pink-coloured quinine
Indonesia:	Watches with date indicators
Iran:	Used razor blades
Iraq:	Rubber balloons
Ireland:	Prison-made goods
Israel:	Sand
Jamaica:	Charms and similar objects
Japan:	Used hay
Kampuchea:	Non-standard thermometers
Kenya:	Milk
Korea:	Ginseng
Kuwait:	Radio sets
Laos:	Artificial honey
Lebanon:	Articles for use in gambling
Liberia:	Football-pool coupons
Libya:	Soap
Liechtenstein:	Commercial horoscopes

Maldives:	Stationery
Mali:	Apparatus capable of making coins
Mauritania:	Poisons not destined for chemists
Mauritius:	Turtle shell
Mexico:	Bonbons
Morocco:	Baby comforters
New Caledonia:	Beverages resembling wine
New Zealand:	'Waterproof economic patent soles' for shoes
Nicaragua:	Footwear
Nigeria:	Lamps or torches
Oman:	Wire
Panama:	Cakes
Papua New Guinea:	Noodles
Poland:	Natural manure
Qatar:	Letters, except one for the addressee
Reunion:	Dead animals
Senegal:	Non-metric weights and measures
RSA:	Flypaper
Spain:	Religious objects such as rosaries
Sudan:	Toy pistols
Surinam:	Nil
Switzerland:	Foreign bank notes
Syria:	Glass
Taiwan:	Camphor
Togo:	Silver Coins
Tristan Da Cunha:	Nil
Tunisia:	Pencils
Turkey:	Binoculars
USSR:	Games of militaristic nature
United Kingdom:	Accounts of horror on disc or film
Venezuela:	Hand fans
Vietnam (SR):	Bones
Yugoslavia:	Cashew nuts

After dinner, the stamp collectors passed round the mints.

S ince I started collecting stamps, I haven't been able to get moving for stamps. It's now got to flood proportions and the faster the main streams flow, the more flotsam and jetsam gets left lying around on the banks, high and dry, doing not much good to nobody.

I'm sure you know the problem. You see a pile of stuff you fancy, space fillers, very reasonable, so you haggle a bit, get the old miser down, then rush home gloating, only to find you have half of them already. And the other half are so tatty you can't bear to give them album room.

Or you decide to pursue a new speciality. I have an album of covers, most of them cheap Victorian stuff, but with no pattern to them, no rhyme or reason, but I quite liked them when I got them about a year ago. It's all far too broad and general, so I've now decided I'm going to concentrate instead on covers with Cumbrian post marks. So there. But what do I do with all this other stuff I have? I could re-do my will, leaving them to Raife Wellsted of the National Postal Museum, but I'm sure he's got

"No! It isn't a paper chase!
Thompson has absconded with the Stamp Club swop box!"

more than enough tatty penny lilac covers, thank you very much.

I also do a lot of re-constructing. You know, trying to collect two hundred and forty stamps according to their different lettering. I never seem to have my wants lists with me when I wander into a new stamp shop, and I end up buying endless doubles. What a dumdum.

Then now and again I go really mad and buy a stamp which is not tatty, not even average used, even, dare I say it, VLMM. (In case you are reading this in a shop, looking for a copy of the *Dandy*, that stands for Very Lightly Mounted Mint. And by the way, this is *not* a reading room. Get your money out, you mean beggar.)

With wisdom, one does try to buy a few of the better stamps, doesn't one, which of course is the dealer's oldest ploy in the business. Once they get you caught on that, you can go on for ever. But what do you do with the inferior stuff, those pathetic things you once loved so dearly?

I have acres and albums and drawers of stuff that are now surplus to requirements. I mentioned some time ago how I tried to unload some of the choicer stuff at Sotheby's, and was told to kindly leave the stage. They don't like single lots under £100. And as we all know, your average local stamp shop is in a cash flow crisis situation, as of this moment in time. It's the recession, innit.

But stay. I have good news for all those amateur collectors like me with stamps to spare. We don't really want to make a profit on them, do we, as we stamp collectors are not greedy, being such lovely, generous kindly people. We would rather they found a nice, clean home. Or best of all to be able to swop them for stuff we haven't got.

I know you can join clubs. I'm in the Railway Philatelic Group, though I haven't seen one of their packages recently. I did think of putting some of my swops in the packages, but I couldn't understand the instructions and the paperwork looked enormous.

So what I have done is hire a hall and organise my own Stamp Swop Shop. See. I knew you'd be interested. I gather that in places like Germany every big Philatelic Exhibition has a day on which collectors can come along and swop with each other. Dealers, apparently, were against the idea at first, but gave in when these swop days attracted the biggest crowds of all.

The idea came to me when I learned that my local stamp shop in Hampstead was closing. It was such a centre for young collectors on Saturdays that I thought I'd try to do something to keep stamps alive in our area, and also give a facility for people like myself with spare stamps to swop or sell.

I've booked Burgh House in New End Square, right in the middle of Hampstead village, near the tube. This is a famous historic house, full of exhibitions and beautiful rooms, and has a licensed buttery which does lunch, teas, coffee. I've persuaded my family to make a day of it, and I'll buy them lunch, if they help on my stall.

It's a completely non-profit making venture. It's costing me £30 for the day, which I think is a bargain, and I'm taking an advert in the *Ham and High*, the local paper, which will cost another £20. I'm offering 10 tables to people trying to *sell* stamps, or postcards or similar collectable things, at £5 for the day. A few dealers and semi-professionals have taken some of the tables already. Those wanting to swop can have space for nothing. Have I gone mad? Will no one turn up? Watch this space . . .

Travelling Post-office.

I got to my Stamp Fair at 9.45 on Sunday morning, to find nine dealers already there, loaded down with cases and boxes, all wanting to get in, all asking me dopey questions, as if I knew the answer to anything, as if I've done this sort of thing before. They all thought that having paid me their measly fiver I was their property for the day.

We had to get the tables out of the WC, so that led to a lot of moans and groans, huffing and puffing, but at last I got them all settled. Or so I thought. Someone didn't like his table and wanted nearer the door. Another said it was too hot. Then it was too cold. Then the Curator of the House came screaming at me cos some stupid stamp dealer had pinned his bargain notices all over some precious paintings. I dunno.

I had brought my own stuff with me, a case full of lovely Q.V. swops, covers and cards, stamps and bundles, but I was so busy being a nanny to one and all that I hadn't time to lay out my stall. The public was there even before we were ready, which was nice. Well, two of them.

I got my daughter Flora to take the 10p admissions. I'd decided at the last moment to charge as I realised I'd spent several pounds on postage, telling the world about the Fair, although the object of the Fair was to be non-profit making. We took about £10, which meant that over a hundred people turned up, counting children, half price.

It wasn't till about lunchtime that I at last found time to set up my stall, which was the scruffiest in the room. Everybody kept on coming up and asking me if I did Poland, then it was France, or first day covers. Nobody seemed to want my GB Victorian stuff. You name it, I hadn't got it. But at least there was a continual stream of customers, so I hoped all the other stalls were doing good business.

Then, a little boy came up and wanted to buy a 1925 Wembley mint set which I'd priced at £25, a bargain, honest. He was the son of a friend of mine so I tried to say it wasn't for sale. It seemed rotten to take money from a kid, even though it was a bargain, already. I said what about these 1841 Penny Red Covers, trific value at 40p each, but he'd set his heart on the Wembleys. I let him have them for £20, without him trying to get me down. I'll never be the next Stanley Gibbons.

Just before closing time there was a mad rush and some old

ladies started scrambling in my Swop Box. I'd thrown in some modern stuff, stamps torn off envelopes, and had a notice saying take out as many as you like, as long as you put in the same number. Until then, nobody had seemed interested. By the end of the day, it had emptied. How come? According to my maths, I should have ended up with the number I'd started with. Well, Stanley probably made similar mistakes in his early days.

I don't usually consider myself the dealer's friend, but I have to admit I now sympathise with them more. The amount of boring people you have to put up with, droning on about amazing bargains they nearly got, but didn't, or how they used to have amazing stamps, but haven't now. There is no escape. They are the customer and they've got you trapped.

You daren't leave the stall, in case there's a rush, or even worse, someone might pinch something, though my stall was in such a mess I didn't know what I had.

It's like footballers at the Cup Final. They dream about it, before and after, but on the actual day they are in such a daze that they don't really take it in. I'd worried about my Fair for weeks, but the day itself went in a flash. It was a fascinating experience, and I hope you will try it, wherever you are. There must be a cheap hall you can hire and enough friends, or contacts, amateurs or professionals (we had half and half), who will take a stall. Everyone has got stuff they would like to sell or swop.

I could have made a profit on the day, if I'd wanted to. The bloke who was the main moaner at the beginning of the day was still moaning at the end, but everyone else was very pleased, having sold between £60 and £100 worth of stamps. They said they would have paid double for their stall. At most Collectors' Fairs the going rate is £10–£20. So on the day, I could have made £50.

The best fun was seeing ten stamp stalls, all in the same room. I wish I could have gone round them all properly, and

---

Does yours need a magnifying glass?

---

examined all their wares, but I was stuck on my draggy old stall. Next time, I'll be a customer. After all, the customer is always right.

The first postmen in a British town were employed in 1680 by William Dockwra for his London Penny Post system. He also introduced the first handstruck postage marks.

Did you go to the Wembley Exhibition? It was really good. I have battle scars on my wallet to prove I went and the pains in my legs, doctor, are still there. Why did I stand up for those five hours? I really went to feast my eyes, to ogle all the goodies, but I ended up getting carried away, seduced by one particular set of riches.

Normally, when I go to Wem-bel-ee, it's my throat which takes a battering. Those two Cup Finals in May were incredible. Wem-bel-ee, Wem-bel-ee. You hear that strangled cry on every football terrace, up and down the country, as some poor, pathetic groups of fans hope once again that this year their team might get to the Cup Final.

We philatelic phans are much more sedate as we wend our

"Lick this for stickability!"

way to Wembley. It was so strange not to have to fight through massive crowds or wade through piles of litter, assaulted by the Hot Gospellers (the sandwich board men, not the girls) or the touts selling dodgy tickets and worst of all, the horrible smell of hot dog stalls which always pollutes every route to Wembley on the day of a big match.

I hope that every collector who went to Wembley for the Big Stamp Day took a brief look at the amazing Empire Stadium. It really is part of our history, postal as well as sporting, as of course our very first commemorative stamps came out in 1924 to celebrate the British Empire Exhibition which used the Stadium, along with many other incredible buildings, all of them long since gone.

The British Philatelic Exhibition was being held at Wembley's new Conference Centre, not in the Stadium itself. It's all very

Stamp collectors are never unhinged.

modern and posh, a bit like a Hilton Hotel, and I was half worried at first I'd come to the wrong building. How could we humble little stamp collectors justify having such a massive place to show our wares? I felt rather proud as I walked up the steps.

Sitting at home, alone with one's albums, alone with one's thoughts, one can feel rather forlorn, as if cast away on an emotional desert island. I wish I'd brought my family with me so I could have said look at all the lovely happy people. See, I'm not the only nutter on the beach.

There were about fifty assorted stamp stalls, mostly arranged upstairs, along a sort of gallery, with the exhibitions displayed downstairs. It was only the third really big stamp exhibition I've been to in my philatelic life.

I went to Stampex at Olympia, where the parking was hell and then something equally big at the Chelsea Flower Show halls in Victoria, which was even heller for parking and completely baffling as they were using two halls on different sites. My memory of each show is one of bewilderment. I was a virgin collector then. I couldn't work out what was going on and wandered round in a dream, occasionally asking a stall-holder, when there was a break in the crowds, if they had any stamps. You know, well, British stamps. Eh, well, any really. I felt such a fool.

Now I have so many specialist collections on the go that I was able to reel off a dozen specific wants and sound terribly knowledgeable.

I did have moments of being nauseated by it all. There are so many stamps. And so many collectors spending so much money. And then the winning exhibitions, those who have Gold Lamé Medals for Bravery and Half Bronze Trophies for being millionaires and Very Wonderful Plates for being a Grand Prix, well, it puts you off.

I was impressed by most of the dealers. You get the chatty ones, talking loudly with some of their regulars, cracking awful jokes, swapping semi-insults, the extroverts who should really be in Petticoat Lane. Then there are the very quiet ones, heads down, sorting away, but their eyes missing nothing. They hope at least they'll miss nothing being nicked. All of them were quick and efficient, knowledgeable and helpful, almost high on the excitement of it all.

Most of the fans, like me, seemed to be in their own private world, sorting through boxes and displays in a trance. I queued up behind one bloke of about thirty who was spending pounds and pounds on some Victorian covers. He was obviously a regular and the dealer was thanking him loudly for his support, urging him to buy even more. 'I'd give it all up tomorrow,' said the man wearily, 'in exchange for a good sex life.'

I didn't spend a great deal, honestly. (That's in case my wife reads this.) Till I came to a stand which had some old Wembley postcards. They were so fascinating, showing all the 1924 and 1925 Exhibition Pavilions, many with Wembley stamps on. Well, I fell. I bought about fifty in all. I didn't mean to. Here we go again. Another collection started. Wem-bel-ee . . .

Jim Dutton of Leatherhead has got a problem. He collects Irish pre-war definitives and has always wondered why it is that the 2p value appears to be referred to in the singular. For example, on the stamps, you get 1 pingin, 2 pingin, yet 3 pingins, 4 pingins, 5 pingins, etc. Why should 2p not take the plural form?

'Some years ago I did ask an Irish stamp dealer to explain the mystery. "This would take a long time to explain," so he told me. "If you could converse in Gaelic, it would be much easier to understand than by direct translation to English."

'I remain in the dark, totally obscured to this day.'

Stamp forgeries are a faking nuisance.

The Stamp

It travels through the countryside,
And over water too,
To do its special duty
For the Inland Revenue.
Commemoratives and Definitives
Works of art in miniature —
The Stamp, the true Ambassador
Whether of Britain or Tuvalu.

It gives pleasure to the thousands
Who collect it as a hobby.
It's instrumental in providing
Business ventures in the lobby
Of hotel, in exhibition,
Where the people flock to see it.
It's a source of inspiration
For the Student and the Poet.

Illustrations they are endless,
From the simple to exquisite.
Competitions are provided
To find out who's best to do it.
From the Lord who sits in Parliament,
To the gipsy in his camp,
For them both to post a letter,
They have first to lick the stamp.

*(This contribution is from Joseph Carey of Caversham,
Reading. Could he be the new McGonagall?)*

Stamp collectors do it on their own.

Ten reasons why I hate stamps. Before you demand your money back, remember that in all pleasure there is pain, in all passion there is fury, in all love there is hate. Now read on. If you dare.

1) They are so worthless. Really, what is the value of such stupid little scraps of paper, most of which are dirty and worn and scruffy, at least they are in my collection. Tou might go for mint Penny Blax. The rest of us have to make do with v. v. v. used. But all the same, when it comes down to it, they are valueless bits of paper. You can at least melt down gold coins, and sell them, or chop up Chippendale chairs and burn them, or take down those First Editions and read them. Stamps are nothing, unless they're stamps.

2) There are too many of them. Close your eyes for a moment. Count to five. Right, ten thousand Chinese have been born but ten million stamps have also been rushed on to the market, most of them from islands you've never heard of.

3) There has always been too many of them. I despair when I think of all the stamps I haven't got. Who's got them? It's not fair. You tell me there were sixty-eight million Penny Blacks printed, but I don't believe a word of it. Show me them. Why have I got so few?

4) The prices. My God, the prices. Yet all the stamps I bought when I seriously became a collector are now worth less than I paid for them. What have I done? Let's not talk about prices.

5) I can't pass on my pleasure to other people who are not stamp collectors. What a shame. I would dearly love to get my family interested, but their eyes go glazed. Stamps are a complete mystery, to those not interested in stamps. If I'd chosen to collect paintings instead I could at least have had some things for other people to enjoy and admire.

6) Even amongst stamp lovers, and where are you all hiding, it is also hard to pass on the pleasure in one's own special interest. They listen, dutifully, waiting for a pause, while you tell them about your Wembley 1925 postal markings. Then they rush in with their amazing knowledge of the Estonian Provisional Period of 1918–20. Two monologues ensue, when all I long for is a dialogue.

7) I get depressed when I see good stamps. Have you ever been to the National Postal Museum? or seen the Gold Medal

Exhibits at stamp shows? I get very fed up. All that time and worry and money on my pathetic little specimens.

8) I keep on buying stamps I've already got. What a fool I am.

9) I keep on having to change albums, re-arrange the collections, decide on another way of displaying my treasures. So I look at the accessories counter, and does that help, does it heckers. It just confuses me. Plastic science has taken over and left me behind.

10) My eyes are getting weaker, doctor. The more I go into my chosen specialities, the more I am forced to count the perforations, investigate invisible plates or do myself an injury looking for non-existent water marks. I'm now saving hard for an X-ray machine to analyse the gum. Should I carry on or take up something easy like hang gliding?

T en reasons why I love stamps. If you were alive a few moments ago you will remember that I was moaning on about all the draggy aspects of stamp collecting, how I sometimes hate them, sometimes, well if you read it last time, I need not repeat myself. This time I'll do a *volte face*, or is it a *tête bêche*? I never know. I don't collect French stamps.

1) They are so small. That might sound like a negative asset, but in the days when I collected other things, like motorway juggernauts and second-hand Concordes, I had nowhere to put them. Stamps are so portable. You can post them, pack them, display them, hide them, eat them, so quickly and so easily.

2) There are so many of them. Sand grains on the shore, pebbles on the beach, humans on the planet, or stamps of Great Britain? Which is the most numerous? I don't know. I just ask the questions in this house. You're the clever ones. But here's a fact for you. The population of GB today is smaller than the number of Penny Blacks produced in 1840. And that was just one issue. Today, billions and billions of stamps are being produced, just from this one little island. More than enough fun for anyone.

3) They are all so different. What this means is that even an absolute beginner can amass a collection which is unique. The permutations are limitless. We can all be experts. I have definitely the world's greatest collection of Penny Reds with the letters HD on, all of them torn and scruffy and horrible. Nobody else would want them, but that's not the point. They are mine, all mine.

4) They are cheap. Yes, I know they are also expensive, but what else can you collect for absolutely nothing which will provide hours of fun for healthy boys and at the same time start becoming valuable? I save every stamp which comes through my letter box, either for myself or for the school's stamp stall at the next jumble. Gibbons are selling used £1 stamps at 85p each, so their latest catalogue says, and they even price all those boring commemorative stamps at 25p each. I know you

couldn't sell yours for that price, but every stamp that comes through the door has a notional value, which grows all the time.

5) Even the most valuable stamps can be cheap. A poor example of almost every stamp, even the rarest, comes within the range of most collectors. Space fillers, they're called, and the various adjectives dragged out by dealers to catch unwary punters must be examined with caution. One man's Fine Used is another man's Definitely Grotty. All the same, you want a Penny Black, then fine, here's a horrible one, but it is the genuine article, well, part of the genuine article, minus a few margins, in fact a few acres, but it is your actual P. Black, yours for only £5, I'm giving them away today.

Imagine collecting Rembrandts. Could you go into a Bond Street Gallery and ask for any Rembrandt space fillers, tatty ones to complete your set, you don't mind used ones, even with missing perfs or thins? No chance.

6) They're so educational. I now know where Umm Al Qaiwain is. I'm not telling though. I hope if I keep it a secret it will go away and stop bothering me any more with its rotten issues. But stamps do make me go out and find a few fascinating facts about the big wide world.

7) They're so rich and diverse. You can go simply for pretty pictures, as I do with my thematic collection of railway stamps, or you can go for something baffling, like the plating of Penny Blacks.

I was in Gibbons the other day and I asked an expert, just in passing, to plate a tatty Black I'd just bought. Even he had to bring out this huge book before he could manage it. They should have Ph.Ds in philately.

8) They're so exciting. It's hard to prove this to outsiders, but when you track down that final stamp in the set or the sequence or the reign or whatever dopey thing it is you're after, then the old hands tremble and the tweezers twitch and the heart pounds and, really, I think that perhaps I should take up something less exciting.

9) They're so relaxing. Having calmed down, and avoided that seizure, you then open the new ones and settle yourself comfortably. The hours pass, the days fly, the weeks go by.

Lost in the wonderful world of stamps, all cares forgotten. Much better than valium.

10) They are indeed a drug. Any political party who will put them on the National Health will have my vote. Four million sufferers can't be wrong.

The oldest post office in Britain still in its original building is at Sanquhar, Dumfries.

I t was a old Victorian school hall and I arrived a bit late, which was rather rude, as this was my first visit to their Stamp Club. Even so, there was nobody there. I went out and waited. Perhaps they would all arrive with a rush. It might even end up standing room only. So I went back in again, and took off my coat and sat on a seat at the front.

Two old ladies came tottering in, not a day under eighty, and started squabbling over a tea urn. Then two old men arrived, not a day under eighty-five, and started squabbling over who would make the Thank You speech afterwards.

A very bossy young lady, a chicken of seventy, came in and started opening the post very officiously, laying out stamp catalogues and lists and notices on a little table. I went over to look at them, giving a little cough, hoping someone would say: 'Hello, you must be the new member.' They all had their coats on. That was it. Must be the secret sign. That's how they know you're one of them. So I put my coat on again and sat down, only to see them all taking their coats off.

A man with a walking stick and a foreign accent hobbled in and they all immediately addressed him as Mr President, how are you Mr President, it's my turn to make the Thank You speech, Mr President, and Mr President, *she* gave out the tea last week.

The meeting was due to start at 7.30, by which time there were seven of us gathered together, including the Guest Speaker.

The bossy lady Secretary stood up and began reading out the Minutes of Meeting 743, and I thought Oh no, I'm going to be here till next week, but then someone proposed the minutes be taken as read. At long last we were ready to start Meeting 744.

The guest speaker spent the first five minutes apologising in advance in case he was going to bore any of us. I was about the only person attending, as the two rival Thank You Speakers were making notes and the Tea Ladies were knitting, but both eyeing the clock, ready for a quick dash. Everyone else appeared to be asleep.

It had looked an interesting evening in the club's printed programme, more exciting than some of their other monthly meetings. I was glad to have missed 'Disaster Mail Postal Marks left by Alsatians' given by the local vet. 'Full Frontal Franking' might have been quite good, but it was during the Soho Provisional Period of 1830, a rather boring time, I always think, philatelically. Soho wasn't really exciting until Obliterators, Rubbers, Hand Stamping, More to Pay and of course the Downy Head Display.

Coming soon, so the programme said, was the local head-

Stamp collectors do it with tweezers.

---

mistress on 'Feminists on Stamps' and then the Vicar was down to give a display of 'Camp Post'. That might be good.

Tonight, the Guest Speaker, in real life a bus driver, was showing us his collection of 'Railway Stamps'. I found it absolutely fascinating. I never knew when and where the

"I wouldn't mind betting she uses stamp hinges!"

world's first railway stamp was issued, the first stamp ever with a train on, did you know? Go on, guess. New Brunswick, 1860, a little one-cent purple. See, that proves I was listening.

He had arranged his collection alphabetically, going through each country in turn. Apart from railway stamps, he also had railway postcards, railway maps from each country, or photographs of the railway pioneers. When he couldn't get a suitable stamp to illustrate a country's trains, he did a bit of verbal fiddling.

He showed us one stamp with two black crows on, or so it appeared, which didn't seem to have anything to do with trains. He explained that they weren't crows but two choughs.

(Chuff, chuff. Get it?) Oh yes, fiendishly ingenious, these stamp experts.

At half time, which was when he got to the letter K, tea was given out, or rather thrown out, as the two ladies were in their own competition, determined not to be beaten. They were so exhausted that they fell asleep during the second half. I think I was the only one awake when the speaker finally got to Z for Zaire and Zambia, both of which have lovely railway stamps, you should have seen them, very colourful.

The two Thank You gentlemen had also nodded off completely, so I stood up and said it had been a rail pleasure to listen to him, ho ho. The noise of the Speaker laughing politely woke up the Gents who were absolutely furious. A New Member, daring to say Thank You. Let me tell you, young man, we've been in this Club for forty-three years...

Next meeting, it's the President's Night, when he has the pick of the ladies, or is it the pick of the old packets. Then they all get auctioned. I'll be there.

It's so reassuring to think that all over the country, even as we sit here now, little groups of stamp lovers are meeting together, communing through the brotherhood of stamps.

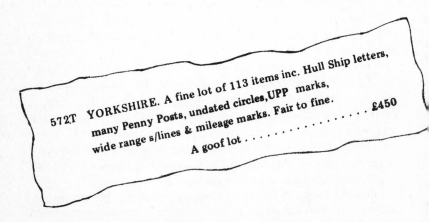

572T   YORKSHIRE. A fine lot of 113 items inc. Hull Ship letters, many Penny Posts, undated circles, UPP marks, wide range s/lines & mileage marks. Fair to fine. A goof lot £450

From the auction catalogue of William Carson of Ayr, April 23, 1983. Yes, another goofy misprint...

Have gum, will travel.

As you know, I collect old bonds as well as stamps and if you're sitting comfortably I'll tell you a sorry tale. Sorry, I'll just stick to the tale. You can decide on the sorrow.

It all started two years ago when I was in Gibbons, poking around, and I saw a sign saying Old Bonds and Shares so I wandered into this department and found a speciality I never knew existed. I bought some old American railway bonds, mainly from the nineteenth century, issued by railway companies which have long since gone or been taken over.

When I heard recently that Gibbons were getting out of bonds, I bought a job lot of stuff they were selling, or had been trying to sell, at £25 each or over. Clever old me, I thought, having got my lot for about £10 each.

I bought many duplicates of course, as I was buying their complete stock of some of the bonds, so I decided to sell the spare ones at auction.

Over the last two years, I have bought lots of stamps stuff at three main auction houses — Sotheby's, Phillips, and James of Norwich. So I thought I would honour them with my custom, now that for the first time in my life I was seriously trying to sell.

I sent each auction house an identical bundle of 36 railway bonds, mainly American but with a few GB. I didn't bother to ask their terms, or even to read the small print in all their catalogues which clutter up my room, which of course was lazy and rather stupid.

I didn't want to make a profit, just get some of my money back, as I was worried that could mean paying tax or VAT or other disgusting three-letter words.

I posted them in July and they appeared in the respective auction house catalogues in October. There were great differences in their estimates for bonds which were absolutely identical. For example, a Baltimore and Susquehanna Rail Road bond of 1838 was estimated by Sotheby's to be worth £40–£60. They got £65 for it, so that was good. James estimated the same bond at £20, but got £40. Phillips, for some reason, lumped it together with another bond from a completely different railway company, and put their estimate at £40–£50. They got only £21 for the two, which I thought was a rotten result, though somebody got a bargain.

The total proceeds from the three different salerooms were as follows. Sotheby's did best and took off least. They realised £298 on my bonds and charged me only a flat 10 per cent commission on the total sold, plus a little bit of VAT, which came to £35.42, and meant I received a cheque for £262.58.

James realised £207, charged me £78.22 (this was commission at 15 per cent on each lot, with a minimum of £2, plus VAT, plus insurance) which left me with only £128.78.

Phillips realised £210, took off £81.98 for charges (commission was 10 per cent but the minimum on each lot was £5, plus insurance, plus VAT) which left me with £128.02.

So what's the moral, folks? Sotheby's, going by these figures, is by far the best place to sell. James' and Phillips' total charges came to around 33 per cent which staggered me, but it was my own fault. I had not realised they had a minimum charge for lots sold, or unsold, which means if you're selling cheap things, you pay very dearly.

I'm not accusing any of them of being extortionate. I'm sure my little bundles were a waste of their time and overheads. The market in bonds has collapsed and Sotheby's, who got the best prices for me, say they have no more bonds sales planned.

I just feel sorry for myself, wasting my own time and money. On average, my return on all the bonds was £5 each — which is about half what I paid for them. I must be mad. But at least I now understand the mechanics of auction sales a bit better. I've learned my main lesson. Stick to being a buyer not a seller. Everyone loves a buyer.

In Finland, one of the leading Helsinki stamp dealers is called 'Superbum'.

I can feel a new collection coming on but before I tell you about it, here's a question for you. I always do this when I sense the urge arising in the old limbs, the sap surging, the gum moistening at the edge. I keep interrupting myself in the hope that it will go away and leave me alone. Anyway, I want you to identify the source of a line from an advertisement which has been sent to me by A. Yarrow (BPF) of Harlow, Essex. He just cut it out and posted it to me. Wasn't that kind?

'The collector should be held under a running tap and gently squeezed between the fingers.'

You've got between now and the end of the next page, and no cheating, I am watching, to work out what sort of collector is being described

My new passion is all the fault of Ron Greenwood and his lads. If only Paul Mariner hadn't got that jammy goal against Hungary at Wembley I would never have thought of taking up football stamps. I'm already making lists of things to look out for during the World Cup, or not look out for. If it becomes as dopey as Lady Di and all those ten million lumps of rock in the middle of nowhere which produced Royal Wedding stamps then I'll probably give up before I've even started.

I've already scribbled a check list. I really must control myself. I was holding on for Directory Enquiries, the hours went by, the weeks flew, and with my ear cocked I was idly thumbing through *Stamps of the World* with my free limbs. I honestly didn't know I was doing it. It's very hard to manage. You know how heavy that volume is. I mean the big one.

I managed to look up Uruguay, which was quite difficult as I kept getting Vathy, a town on the island of Samos, where in 1893 there was a French post office, now closed. So it says here. I didn't want that, did I. They never hold a World Cup there. Then I got Upper Yafa. I'm not making any of this up. Upper Yafa was apparently somewhere in South Arabia, for half an hour, back in 1967, during which time it managed to shove out a few stamps. Some countries do get their priorities right.

Eventually, with my one free hand, I found Uruguay. Hurrah. They held the First World cup there in the 1930s and yes, they did, no they didn't, curses, they didn't issue one stamp to celebrate the World Cup. What a stupid country. Glad I don't collect their stamps. Here's me, all panting to start work on the world's best collection of football stamps, then Uruguay lets me down.

I'll just have a quick look at Italy. They staged the second World Cup finals in 1934. That's more like it. Trust the Eye Ties. They shoved out nine stamps from the 1934 World Cup, if I'm reading all these Stanley Gibbons hieroglyphics correctly. Well done Italy. That will do nicely. Tomorrow morning, I'll honour some stamp shop with my presence and start my amazing collection of footbally stamps, working my way from Italy 1934, to France 1938, Brazil 1950, Switzerland, 1954, oh I needn't go on. Don't want *everybody* collecting football stamps.

That reminds me. I already have a packet of football stamps somewhere in this house. Two years ago, when I was trying to get my son Jake to take up a worthwhile interest in life, something really positive instead of helping old people across the road or running soup kitchens, I suggested he should collect football stamps. I got a packet for £1, one of those ones covered in cellophane which are murder to rip off and are a great disappointment when you do as you then discover all the rubbish stamps from the rubbish countries lurking underneath which you never suspected were there. He never even opened them. S'boring. That was all he said. I must have put them somewhere. They could be my starter pack for my new and wonderful collection. I'll look for them later.

Oh, this is going to be good fun. Between now and the World Cup I should be able to get together quite a lot of football stamps. Should I stick to World Cup stamps or go for any old footballers on any old stamps? Decisions, decisions.

Haven't I seen a rather nice-looking Monaco stamp which has Wembley stadium on it? I think it was triangular. Or is my mind wandering. Next time I make a phone call, I'll look it up in *Stamps of the World*. Never let it be said that I *waste* my time on *my* stamp *collections*.

Now for the answer to my question. The collector referred to in the advert was Cadnit's fur collector. You know, that sort of wire mesh thing you put in a kettle and it collects all the horrible stuff. We have one we use in our electric kettle. Do you think Mr Cadnit will now send me a free supply? For giving him a plug.

Thank you, Mr Yarrow. Jake says that BPF stands for Bloody Philatelic Fool. He said it. Not me. I'm not allowed to swear.

Swap stamps not wives.

W hen did it all start exactly?
I don't really want to talk about it, right. I know you're a doctor and all that, just wanna help, but it's too late, see. Leave me alone.

Quite. I do understand. But there are ways we can help addicts these days, even incurables, which is what you say you are. Did you begin in the usual way as a boy?

Yeh, gum sniffing, that's wot started it off, spose. That's when I got my first fix.

It sounds as if you became un-hinged from an early age. We do have a lot of cases like this. Believe me, you are not alone.

I just couldn't get enough, know what I mean. I used to lick the backs of them for hours. I knew it was stupid, like. When I ran out of hinges, and all the late-night stamp shops were closed, I used to lick the backs of the stamps themselves. Stupid, I know, don't tell me. God, I wish I had them all now. It was the taste, you see, and the smell of the gum. Original gum, that's what I like best.

Didn't your parents try to help you?

Oh yeh. I must have driven them potty. I knew they were worred about me. It affected me school work, see. Failed all me GCEs. I used to hang around these back streets round the Strand. I was scared at first, all these older people, talking this strange way, doing funny things to each other with these instruments I'd never seen before.

When did you get your first tweezers?

Me birthday. I made them get me a pair. I said I'd be forced to steal a pair if they didn't. I knew this boy at school. I'd seen his, locked up in his desk. That was it, really. I never used my hands after that. I did it all with tweezers. It was painful at first, till I got the hang of it. Look, here's the marks. They're still there. You can get a hell of a nip, if they go in the wrong way.

Quite. There's no need to go into details. Tell me, is there history of addiction in your family?

Me dad said it wasn't his side of the family. They'd all been steady people, nothing stronger than fretwork. It was me Mum's uncle. I found out he'd got a few packets, hidden away in the back of an old cupboard. I used to look at them when he didn't know, under the blankets in bed.

"Do you think we ought to pander to his specialist interest in gum flavours?"

Didn't he try to help, if he'd been a sufferer himself?

Oh yeh, he was a good bloke, rest his soul. An omnibus got him.

Tragic. These omnibuses do get out of control. We've had a lot of complaints at the clinic about them, especially the Royal Wedding ones. I fear the World Cup ones will do an equal amount of damage. I'm hoping the Government will have a word with the Crown Agents.

It was me uncle that got me off the gum sniffing. He introduced me to Hawids. I started on the 30mm ones then I went on to the 40mms. It was like a new world. Then I discovered Hagners. They were really wild. They were difficult to get at first, as they come from Sweden, then I found a good supplier in Chichester.

When did you move on to the hard stuff?

Blues, you mean. Well, I'd started on the soft stuff, the Reds. Anyone can get them. They're everywhere. But you get used to them after a while, know what I mean? The sort of effect doesn't last long.

I'm told that Blues are very expensive these days.

Bloody expensive, mate, even down the back streets, but I found a few mail-order firms, under plain cover, say no more.

How did you get the money?

I did what most people do. Bit a trading, didn't I. This fella supplied me with FDCs. I had to push them round the kids, on commission, and then he slipped me a few of the specials. Obliterators. They blow your mind. Duplex, I often got a few of them. I'm not as keen on definitives. They don't do nuffink for me.

Are those perforations you have there in your hand?

Yeh. They affect your eyes in the end. The world sort of starts swimming. You can't concentrate. You have to count them, see, 14 or 16, and that's what does it.

Yes, you are in a bad way. All I can suggest is that you take these anti-phosphorus tablets. If that doesn't work, it will have to be Dr Machin's clinic. You know what that means. Cold showers every time you feel the urge coming on. Next please.

The most northerly post office in Britain is at Haroldswick on the island of Unst in the Shetlands.

Roy Thomson's remark about commercial television was a bit of an exaggeration, saying it was a licence to print money. After all, you still have to go and create something. More or less. He should really have been talking about postage stamps.

In 1981, the Post Office made at least £15 million in extra revenue just by printing special stamps. They put various prices on little bits of paper, and sold them. They also, of course, did a lot of work during the year. They issued five thousand million stamps in all, worth £435 million, and the vast majority ended up on letters which had to be carried about

"_How_ big did you say the new River Fish stamps are?"

by postmen. But £15 million came from stamps sold by their twenty-six philatelic counters around the country, for collectors to put straight into their stamp albums. The total sum taken from collectors was probably nearer £20 million.

If you collect British stamps, you like to have every new one. If you live here, you need only go to the nearest post office. If you live abroad, your local stamp dealer can supply you, usually for about twice the cover price. The more new stamps a country can push out, the more money it can make.

Unless you've been on Mars, you must have noticed that every few months nowadays the Post Office brings out some funny-looking new stamps. They have seven planned next year and as usual there will be special first-day covers, presentation packs and other excitements to go with them.

Britain was rather late in getting into the field of commemorative stamps and its output is still comparatively modest. Generally, the less important a country, the more stamps it puts out. By the same token the gaudier the stamps, the more corrupt the government.

It may have been only a coincidence, but Britain dramatically increased its output of special stamps in 1963, when in many ways it finally declined as a world power. It was the year in which De Gaulle said *non*, we don't want you in the EEC, and the year in which we effectively lost Rhodesia, Nyasaland, Kenya, Nigeria, Zanzibar and other bits of red on the world globe.

Some countries appear to exist almost entirely by their postage stamps, and they are now experiencing the law of diminishing returns. As a collector of railway stamps, I always send

A new issue of stamps appeared in 1983 from the island of Niuafo' Ou, an island in the Tonga group with a population of a thousand. It is also known as Tin Can Island and is famous for its unique postal service which began in 1882. Mail was sealed in empty tin cans, originally old kerosene cans or biscuit tins, and carried to and from the island by swimmers. In the 1920s the then postman, Charles Ramsay, became well known as the 'Swimming Mailman of the South Seas'. In 1931 the service was discontinued after one of the swimmers had been eaten by a shark...

back to the dealer anything from Ajman, Umm-Al-Qaiwan or Fujeira. I now know where they all are, but I don't want any more of their stamps.

Our Post Office must therefore tread a fine line, as it tries to increase its philatelic income from collectors like me. If it pushes things too far, the goose will stop laying.

In the old days, when we ruled the waves, British stamps only ever had the monarch's head. The first British commemorative stamp was for the Wembley Exhibition of 1924. There were just two, at a penny and a penny-halfpenny, which can now be worth up to £23. After that there were occasional special stamps to celebrate things like postal centenaries (1940) or the Coronation (1953).

In 1963, when the Post Office changed its policy, there were six special issues — Freedom from Hunger, Paris Postal Conference, Nature Week, Lifeboats, Red Cross and Trans-Pacific Telephone Cable. Guess which is worth most today?

According to the Stanley Gibbons catalogue, the best buys that year were the Paris Postal Conference — the 6d mint stamp is now worth £4; and the Red Cross 1s 6d, now worth £7. You would have lost money, thanks to inflation, if you'd invested in most of the other 1963 special issues.

One can only assume that the main reason why some issues are now worth a lot more than others is that fewer were sold at the time. You have to guess which will be least popular. The Post Office doesn't reveal how many of each stamp it is printing.

All the same, judging by the catalogue prices of recent issues, most people win. The Post Office makes a fortune and the dealers do very well. Stanley Gibbons is already offering *every* special issue from 1980 at around twice the cover price. You must remember the special 12p Queen Mother stamps for her 80th birthday. Some post offices are probably still selling them. Gibbons are now offering used versions for 25p each. So dig them out of the waste paper basket quickly. Naturally, as an ordinary collector, you can't sell your stamps for anything like that, but they still have a value.

On the whole, however, modern commemorative stamps are not good investments. You should put your money into good Victorian stamps, if you really want to invest. But they're a cheap and interesting hobby. They are unlikely ever to be worth *less* than you paid for them. And if you buy every one, which is what the Post Office would like, then over the years many will certainly increase in value.

Some exciting new stamp books which the National Philatelic Society has acquired, according to a list in the *Stamp Lover* magazine for October 1982.

Constant Plate Varieties of the Canadian Small Queens by Hans Reiche

A Large Queen's Report by Hans Reiche

The Early Commonwealth Period and the Kangaroo by the Australian Post Office

The Postal History of Goole by Sedgewick and Ward

The 1913–1914 Recess Printed Series and the King George V Sideface and Pictorial Definitive Stamps by the Australian Post Office

The Story Behind the 2½d Surcharge of 1941 by J. G. Rodger of the Philatelic Society of Fiji

Fig. 393. Senf's Ganzsachen-Aufbewahrungs- heft (geschlossen).

I've been thinking of giving up my subscription to the Philatelic Bureau in Edinburgh. I took it out three years ago, believing that as a stamp collector I should help the lads along, poor things, they need all the pennies they can get, which of course is now a good laugh as the Post Office makes millions out of wee collectors.

I used to have all first day covers sent as well as the presentation packs but they slapped VAT on the covers so I cancelled them. I still get the new issues in their little plastic folders, all artfully designed and packaged, but I don't think I've opened them for months. All that clever writing inside, and I never read any of it.

I can never understand whether I owe them money or not. They have their own form of money, up there in sunny Edinburgh, at least according to their computer which spews out endless notes and invoices in blue ink. They appear to have charged me £1.270 for the Darwin stuff which leaves me with a credit of £16.875. I fear it just needs one slip on the blue ink and they could be round at the back door demanding £16 million from me.

I'm not too upset by the design of the Darwin stamps. I've enjoyed reading all the letters in *The Times* from Disgusted Tunbridge Wells saying the stamps are the worst ever. They might turn out to be a good investment, if you keep them long enough. I should think they must be selling badly, though the Post Office will never admit this until years after it's all over. If not many get shifted, then the ones that are bought might increase in value more quickly than the normal commemorative stamps.

I presume that the designer of the stamps got his arm twisted and had to shove on those soppy animals, as our Post Office well knows that thematic collectors love that sort of stuff. It makes good marketing sense. The Post Office after all, is in the business these days of trying to sell things.

What worries me about it all is the lack of subtlety. It's now getting near the point where they're collecting money and we're collecting labels. So you like collecting labels with animals on? Right, sir, here you are. That will be £1.270.

Hunter's first rule of collecting is never collect anything that has been produced to be collected. Things must originally have had a use, even if that use has long since been forgotten. My famous collection of old US railway bonds is pretty genuine, so I like to think, if pretty useless; so is most of my postal history collection.

" This means George will never finish his designs for the Carnivorous Plant set!

You might disagree, as I'm sure you will. Cigarette cards, after all, were produced to be collected and I can see the fun in them, but count me out. I do collect postcards, though, and they conform to my rule.

So should I give up all modern issues if I maintain they are being created simply to be collected?

I was just about to, when through the post this morning from the Crown Agents came a new stamp from Sri Lanka. I enjoy pronouncing its name, now that I've got the hang of it, but I can't say I've ever been passionate about their stamps.

I was bundling it up for the stamp stall at the school jumble when I looked at the design and noticed it was a rather horrid building, the Department of Inland Revenue in Sri Lanka. I examined it carefully and no, the postal boss had not shoved some animals in the corner or butterflies in the margins. Surely there can't be thematic collectors who collect on the theme of tax buildings? Impossible. So, I've decided it must be a pure stamp. They still do exist. There is hope yet for the world. I have decided to carry on. Okay, Edinburgh. You can breathe again.

The largest post office in the world is the head post office in Chicago, USA.

The longest post office counter in Britain is at the Trafalgar Square Post Office in London; it is 185 feet long and contains 33 positions.

The largest sorting office in Britain is in Birmingham.

I was talking recently about thematic collections which you will remember, if you were paying attention, if you were alive, if you can read, oh do get on with it, and as you well know I have several thematic collections of my own, that's if you read this column, are alive, etc.

There's my railway stamps and my football stamps for a start and with a bit of luck that's where it will finish as I just haven't the space on my walls or in my mind for any more. They're both cluttered up with trivia as it is.

So I am wondering what happens out there in the big wide world, what sort of themes are you collecting, hmmm?

I went down to Gibbons in the Strand and asked them, how's business, don't ask me, I've got problems of my own. Don't mess about, I mean what are your best-selling themes?

They very kindly did a bit of research, analysed their sales of sets and special packages, counted up the general enquiries over the counter and then got out the computer, using the fingers on both hands, and came up with the following list of top ten themes. Don't read on. Can you guess which is their number one? I was quite upset. Poor old railways didn't even make the top ten, though football creeps in at number seven under the general heading of sport.

Top Ten Themes

1 Music, 2 Flowers, 3 Animals, 4 Chess, 5 Art, 6 Boy Scouts, 7 Sport, 8 Heraldry/Uniform, 9 Health/Medicine, 10 Birds.

Some of them are pretty wide categories. Music, for example, covers instruments as well as composers. I'm surprised Birds is not much higher, as so many new issues round the world are devoted to Birds, while Chess on the other hand seems far too high.

Our Post Office should do well this year, with the Boy Scout Stamps and Maritime Uniforms. Next year, so I see, we're going to have Fish on stamps (which I suppose you can put under animals); Gardens, which are bound to have flowers in somewhere; and British Regiments. It explains why they were so keen to shove those animals on to the Darwin stamps.

It would be a good test of a designer's ingenuity to create a stamp which incorporates all ten of the most popular themes, though no doubt the Post Office has already thought of that. Some poor artist is probably slaving over a hot drawing board this very minute. You also need to have some sort of anniversary to celebrate, however phoney.

For the World Cup, we could have had Beethoven kicking a football while he adjusts his deaf aid (for Medicine collectors) and feeds flowers to his pet canary while playing chess with Van Gogh who is dressed as a Boy Scout. I think that covers everything. Perhaps we'd better have a dog wearing the Order of the Garter in the background, to cover animals and heraldry.

You think that all sounds completely dopey? You wait. Gibbons also came up with a list of unusual themes which collectors have come into their shop and asked for. Windmills on stamps is apparently quite a growing speciality, as is sugar

Stamp collectors don't stop at traffic lights.

cane on stamps, fossils on stamps, bananas on stamps, waterfalls on stamps and stamps on stamps. Presumably there is even somebody who collects stamps on stamps on stamps.

The other day someone came into Gibbons and wanted camels on stamps, so the assistant rushed around and managed to find a few sets which depicted camels, feeling very pleased with himself.

'They're all *standing* camels,' said the collector. 'I only collect *running* camels on stamps.' And he left the shop, without buying any of them.

Stamp collectors do it between sheets.

Not a week goes by yet I mourn. Not a day goes by but I think of them. Something went out of my life when they passed on. Something strange is happening to this paragraph as if W. Wordsworth or perhaps A. Tennyson had crept upon me to compose an ode *in memoriam* to a world that is no more.

I refer to my local stamp shop. I admit, oh Master, that I have sinned against them, as I have railed against so many stamp dealers and stamp persons and stamp shops. I might even have made fun of them, had sport at their expense. I now plead forgiveness. I knew not what I was doing, oh great Philatelist across the Strand. I will remain your humble collector, if only I can be spared on this occasion.

My local stamp shop finally closed at Christmas. They invited me to farewell drinks, but I never made it. I flail myself at the memory. How could I? Did I really prefer to go and watch Tottenham Hotspur 1, Arsenal 0? Have I no taste, no sense of decency and propriety? Where are my true values?

Worse was to come. I have lost the home telephone numbers of these friends of mine, that noble duo of stamp dealers, we happy few. I have not been able to ring them and apologise, although how could I have done? Tears I would have shed, down that memory-mingling Buzby-bouncing line to Maida

The City of London Philatelic Auction Catalogues are always worth reading, if only because they insist on putting in the full details of even the most irrelevant information. Boxes, for example, in which so many collectors shove their treasures. To you and me, an old box is an old box, but not to the City of London. Here are some examples from just one catalogue, that for March 18, 1983.

Electronic Starbird Box containing mainly South and Central . . . £55

Birds Eye Box containing FDI and Commercial covers . . . £50

Anchor Box contg foreign accum in bundles (1000's) . . . £40

Brown Box contgn duplicated material in stockcards . . . £40

Leather Boxcase contg World Range in albums . . . £60

Flat Box contg World on leaves with good Egypt and China . . . £35

Rothmans Carton contg Europe and Peru mainly in packets . . . £32

Haig Carton contg range of albums . . . £30

Clarks Shoe Box contg World range . . . £27

World in White Shoe Box, early to modern . . . £30

Home Assortment contg C'w range on stockcards . . . £20

Tri-Sure Plug Box contg misc World in packets . . . £20

Mint Symphony Box contgn C'w bundleware . . . £20

Plastic Vanilla Ice Cream Tub contgn World . . . £20

Vale which is where I think they live or is it St John's Wood? I am left, bereft.

For two long years I wended my far from weary way to their little emporium in the middle of Hampstead village, in the heart of Flask Walk. I visited the shrine, come hail or shine, once a week. I engineered my time, my life, around them. I saved it up, like the best bits on the plate.

I would set off at noon across Hampstead Heath and pop my head in before lunch, to say hello, how's business, I'll be back, don't go away, and then my wife and I would choose an amusing place to lunch, during which I'd savour the delights to come, speculate my mind if not my money, anticipate the expenditure of time if not my income.

Then after lunch, while my wife went to the book shop or the clothes shops or on other mundane pursuits, I would spend at least an hour, sometimes more, poring through their treasures, pouring out my soul. I learned so much about stamps. They were my first teachers. Margaret and Eddie became my mentors. Nothing was too much trouble.

I always tried to buy something, though there was no pressure, fabricating new specialisations when they had nothing new in my line. And I always got the price down. Or they threw in some accessories, some more Hagners or Hawids or some such treats. They would advise me what not to buy, point out the imperfections which I could not see, the flaws in the market, the holes in the arguments.

Since Christmas, alas and alack, I have had a postal correspondence with some kindly dealers in various parts of the kingdom, but they might as well be on another planet. Intercourse is not possible by remote control. How can I reveal my intimate thoughts at such a distance?

I now get unsolicited samples which are never what I want. I fly into a fury at having to wrap them all up again, spending a fortune on registering stuff I never even wanted. Worst of all, you can't get the price down. You need face to face contact, full frontal exposure, especially the exposure of the green stuff in one's hot little hands. That makes magic when it comes to arguing the toss and getting down the price.

The Philatelic Promotion Council, or whatever they call themselves, or the Post Office, should set up and subsidise stamp shops in every little local district. We need them. How can we all survive as collectors without human contact with a local stamp shop?

Sometimes, when I lie awake at night, gently weeping into my Windsor album, I think well, Hunt, you did have two years, two wonderful years of harmless pleasure. Think on, Hunt, I say, about what it must be like to live in the *real* wilderness, out in the sticks without a stamp shop anywhere in sight. How do they survive in Wigton?

I passed the premises today. Silly of me, I know. I still haunt that lane, yet I know my love has gone, remembering times passed, recollecting in tranquillity. Can it now be Proust who is trying to get into this paragraph?

Strange workmen were busy inside, putting up trendy shelves, fashionable windows. I fear it is going to be a boutique or even a picture gallery. Is nothing sacred? Give me back my memories.

Exit right, sobbing.

Fig. 87. Landbriefträger in den »Landes«.

I was bewailing the loss of my local stamp shop and how I feel as sick as a perforated parrot and as choked as Stanley Gibbons on a Saturday morning, but here is some good news. Out of decay comes growth, out of death comes life.

I am now building up some mail order contacts, dealers with whom I have a postal intimacy. It's strange how just by reading their catalogues and lists and seeing how they reply and what they specialise in and if they ever add a covering note, that it's possible, bit by bit, to create a personal relationship. I've never met any of them, these half dozen or so little dealers with whom I regularly correspond, but I like to feel some sort of friendship is growing up. If of course you have some money to spend, *everyone* wants to be your chum, but I like to feel that they *care* about the greater good of the stamp-collecting fraternity, not just the filthy money.

I have not seen any of them in the flesh, but I have an image of each sitting at his or her kitchen table, pushing the dirty dishes aside once they see my familiar scrawl come through the letter box with my latest wants, then they rush to see if they have them, humming gently to themselves.

I decided to write to a couple of my regular dealers and ask if they could tell me a bit about themselves, how they began, some of the secrets of the trade. Graham Mann replied immediately from the West Midlands, where he operates from Reddal Hill Road, Cradley Heath, Warley. He is aged thirty, married with three children and became a full-time dealer in August 1980, having spent the previous seven years selling steel for GKN.

He started collecting stamps at the age of four, then gave up in 1970 when he moved from Kent to the Midlands. In 1976, he re-opened his albums and saw that a humble Penny Black he'd paid £1.10s for in 1968 was now retailing at £10. He started collecting again and in 1979 began part-time as a dealer.

'In that first year, as a part-timer, I sold mainly to dealers. It was during the "boom" and you could walk round a fair for an hour or two with a stock book and do quite well.' He worked from home, but when the living-room proved too small, he moved to the bedroom, then his wife Margaret got fed up with

"If I get the subsidised Improvement Loan from the Post Office I might put up a few more shelves for the vegetables and get a new ice lolly freezer."

the bed being covered with catalogues, albums and stock books. Now he rents a one-room office nearby.

He has no staff but occasionally friends who are keen collectors sort out and check items, just for the fun of it. He works six days a week, usually ten to twelve hours a day, and says he makes a reasonable living. About eighty per cent of his material is bought from auctions. 'I use major houses all over the country, but under no circumstances will I buy from houses employing a buyer's premium. I do not expect to pay for the privilege of spending my money.'

His business is mainly postal, like most one-man dealers, and seventy-five per cent of his sales is by post, ten per cent trade, ten per cent fairs and five per cent callers. His monthly list goes to four hundred people and costs him 50p each, including postage. He seems very happy with his life. Bad handwriting is a constant pain, but the only customer really to annoy him was one who returned superb used commemoratives because they had hinge marks.

For those thinking of going into dealing, if only part time, he advises the following. 1) never sell anything you know to be incorrectly described; 2) don't be scared to advertise, if a beginner is going postal, advertising pays in the long run; 3) when buying, be aware that you will have to add a decent profit margin, around a hundred per cent. 'Some things take a devil of a long time to sell'; 4) find a field not covered by everyone else. He specialises in GB line engraved and surface printed good used, with a special service for reconstructers. 'I do love to help people reconstruct, to find their missing plates. That's the joy of being a dealer.'

For collectors, he predicts that the move away from mint to used will continue, that pre-1900 will grow even more as will QV on cover. He has worked out his own chart of the ups and downs in the market since the war from which, so he thinks, he can tell the future. Things were buoyant from 1946–49, flat from 1950 to 1954, improved from 1955 to 60, slow from 1960 to 1962, quite a boom from 1965 to 1969, collapse from 1969 to 1970, boom from 1977 to 1979, and now things are flat once more.

'I reckon that things will take off again from 1986, then go stale in 1990.' You have been warned.

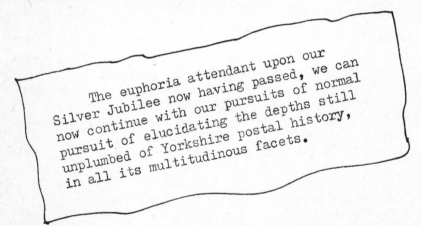

The euphoria attendant upon our Silver Jubilee now having passed, we can now continue with our pursuits of normal pursuit of elucidating the depths still unplumbed of Yorkshire postal history, in all its multitudinous facets.

From the editorial of the Yorkshire Postal History Society's Magazine, March 1983. A fine example of philatelic gobbledegook.

Stick to stamps and get glued to your hobby.

S ettle down, friends, for another homely story of the wheeling dealing world of stamps and how your friendly little local dealer goes about his business. Some of them are quite human.

One day in 1978, two young electrical fitters were chopping away the main circuit boards of a battleship in Portsmouth Dockyard. They got talking, as electrical fitters do, and found they had a common interest in stamps. John Lamonby, then aged twenty-three, had been collecting since 1969, while the other fitter, Steve Allen, then aged twenty-one, had begun only two years previously. They became friends and came up to London together to visit Stampex.

'I remember laughing at the hundreds of punters,' says John, 'who were queuing at the GPO stand to buy the first miniature sheets, the Historic Building ones. I thought they were fools — until three weeks later the price shot up from 53½p to £1.05. It was then that greed took over. We pooled our little savings and sunk the lot in these mini sheets which were £1.45. They then went up so fast that we unloaded at £4.20. Fat profit — almost £3,000.

'Everything was rising, so we went into decimal definitives by the sheet — and promptly lost the lot. Then we went into Christmas booklets, and made a small profit. That was when we decided to become *big dealers*.'

They produced their first mail order list in June 1979, working part-time, and got postal customers by taking one-line adverts in the stamp press. They started with capital of about £1,200 in their joint savings, plus around £1,800 in their joint stock — about £3,000 in all.

'We took our stock to our first stamp fair in Southampton. I thought we would take around £500. Steve felt it would be about £450. We managed £12.57 and came back in tears. We did one fair a week for six months after that, which is an apprenticeship all dealers must go through, but take my advice about fairs — *don't*. Fairs are the hardest way to sell. If you really want to get somewhere, it has to be mail order.'

In their first year, their total turnover was £3,721.52p but it gave them a profit of only £3.50. They went full-time in October, 1981, and now say they are doing a bit better, but still have no staff and work completely from home. Their ambitions are high, however, and they intend to be massive dealers one day. 'We began because we knew which dealers made us angry and which dealers we liked.'

They still get angry when they see fancy prices from the big dealers. 'You just can't sell a Penny Black at £160, but the big dealers try, which is part of the trouble with stamps right now. Gibbons SG prices are ridiculous and give no idea of the true value of a stamp, but I suppose they *must* maintain the prices, or the stamp market would crumble.'

Their monthly list, which they type out themselves, costs them 42p each to produce, including postage. It is distinguished by its wit, which is rare amongst stamp dealers. They always try to get some jokes in somewhere, or little stories and illustrations. To attract customers, so they believe, a list has to be funny, punchy, cheap, and the service must be quick. 'We never charge postage. That's very important.'

Their business is completely mail order, and only GB, and their regulars range from a prisoner in Portsmouth Prison to their bank manager. ('Very lucky.'). Many of their regulars are on the dole. 'You have to remember that collecting is a fixation.'

The Hampstead Stamp Shop used to be run by Mr and Mrs Kon.

The Bath Stamp Shop is run by Mr Swindells.

Somerset Stamp Auctions are run by Mr Grabham.

Their postal customers buy two thirds of every list they send out. 'We don't sell much to dealers. They want something for nothing, as you must surely know. Advertising is vital and you have to get it right. It's expensive, but worth it. We now dwarf the little dealers we grew up with, who still do the stamp fairs, because they didn't advertise.

'We talk together about what stamps we'd personally like to have. We have the hobby in common, with the same outlook as ordinary collectors. We like to think our customers are friends and we're on Christian names terms with most of them.

'If you offer more than the other dealers, and don't charge the fancy prices of the big boys, and work hard, then you'll find no hard times. I think the recession is fading and now is definitely the time to buy. Get hold of good QV at sensible prices and you'll be pounds up in the next two years. I promise you.'

Thank you, Mr Lamonby and Mr Allen. We'll let you know.

Phil, I tell 'ee, gets everywhere...

As soon as I heard about these discount stamp booklets, I went straight round to my friendly local post office to buy some. There was a queue, or it might have been all his relations hanging about, so I decided to come back later. The previous family in the post office, also Indian, gave up recently, alas, as they were terribly helpful, but they got mugged twice and couldn't face it any more. The new bloke has even more children and grannies and aged Ps who help him out, but they are all very charming.

His youngest is a boy wonder, fantastically quick on all the calculations, so I asked him next day about these discount stamps. He hadn't yet heard of them, but he said he would investigate. On my next visit, he explained that you have to cut special coupons out of the newspaper and bring them in.

For a whole week now, I've been examining the *Guardian* with a magnifying glass, inspecting every literal, poking under every misprint, but no Post Office coupon has yet appeared, unless I've missed it.

"It's a sponsored Pack-A-Pillar Box in support of Oxfam!"

How about those lovely Wall's skinless sausages, I said to my lady wife when we were driving to Sainsbury's. I bet the family would love them. Let's stock up, perhaps get a few ton, then I can get for free a whole load of World Cup Football stamps. Certainly not, she said, I hate sausages.

We still have some old packets of Kellogg's Corn Flakes left over. Remember when they did those railway stamps for free? That was very exciting. Loved the stamps. Hated the corn flakes.

I presume that big firms like Kellogg's or Wall's have for years been getting some sort of special discount when they've bought stamps in bulk to give away as a special offer, which of course is only natural. So a little hurrah that ordinary people can now get a discount for bulk buying, or so the rumour hath it.

But will it help the Post Office? Will enough of us actually buy more stamps, just to get the discount? People might change over to a certain beer, if the price came down, but the Post Office has a monopoly so it's unlikely that people will send more letters. They'll save the stamps till they need to use them. We shall see.

I was offered stamps at a discount some years ago in a local stamp shop — ordinary postage stamps, mint GB. The only drawback was that I had to buy £10 worth and they would all be ½p stamps. The explanation seemed very complicated. Apparently a dealer had been tearing apart scores of booklets to get the ones he wanted, and was left with all the halfpenny stamps. I suspected they'd really come off the back of a lorry, or from a post office mugging, so I declined.

I've been back this morning to my local post office and my friendly postmaster showed me a handful of coupons he's already exchanged for booklets, giving the lucky customers a 15p discount on each book. Why don't his bosses just decrease the price of all the booklets? He smiled and said he didn't know.

It would save the Post Office having to buy newspaper space and the the customer having to find the coupons and cut them out. It must also be a right drag for all local post offices, collecting and counting the coupons. The whole process is very mysterious. I can see that the end result might be more convenient for the Post Office, if they end up selling more stamp books, but people might then also buy fewer stamps from the sheets.

I always buy stamp books anyway for their pretty covers, except when new issues came out and I ask for gutter pairs till the counter clerks go spare as they've decimated all their sheets. I suppose by the end of this special offer, I might at last have found one of these newspaper coupons. It could be expensive, if I have to buy other newspapers, just for the coupons.

In the meantime, I'm buying fewer stamps. I'm not going to pay the full price, am I, when somewhere out there people are getting discount. 'Snot fair.

Male stamp collectors need coils.

I n 1975, Stephen Murray was a young carpet layer in Carlisle, working away, bothering nobody, though at the back of his mind was a vague concern about the future.

At the age of twenty-five, he was obviously fit enough for fitting, but what would happen when he got to forty? Would he then be up to all that humping and bending?

His hobby was stamps. Ah, you knew there would a reason for all this. Clever old you. Specially postal history. That was what he liked best and as a part-time occupation he rented a room for £6 a week in Crosby Street, Carlisle, above a health food shop. He worked there on Saturdays and perhaps two other days a week, when he wasn't laying carpets, hoping the good burghers of Carlisle might be interested in buying a few old envelopes and cards which he managed to dig up.

I visited him last week. He now has exceedingly posh premises in Lowther Street, Carlisle's answer to Bond Street. It's a four-storey, Regency building which he owns freehold and from which he runs Globe International and the Carlisle Stamp Centre.

How did he do it? Did he find a stash of fivers under the carpets? His premium bonds came up? A wealthy widow made him an offer he couldn't refuse? If you don't already know the answer, then read on quickly to the next exciting paragraph.

In 1977, he was getting ready to put another load of old rubbish in the incinerator, left-over bits of postal history which he'd gone through for any decent stamp content, when he noticed the name Wordsworth. The address 'Rydal Mount' meant nothing to him, as he hadn't heard of it, but a friend looked up Wordsworth in the public library and found that Wordsworth had indeed lived at such an address. Mr Murray rang Sotheby's. They said stop burning. Come and see us quick. The upshot was the letters were sold for £38,500.

Mr Murray had probably only paid £5 for the letters, at least for an old sack of letters and documents which had been brought in to him. He's not sure where it came from. His practice then was to pay a few quid to people like builders working on a demolition job if they brought him in any old papers which looked interesting. His practice today is much the same, if more sophisticated. With his smart notepaper, three-

"George asked everyone for kiloware last Christmas!"

piece suit, fancy address, impressive references from satisfied customers, he covers the whole northern half of the island, from Inverness down to Chester, contacting old-established firms, such as shipping agents, accountants, lawyers, etc., who might have old store rooms they want cleared.

Nothing as remarkable as the Wordsworth find has come up since — and he is by now heartily sick of the whole Wordsworth saga — and only one in ten of his hauls ever produces anything worthwhile.

I went upstairs to his top floor and saw three rooms full of sacks, waiting to be properly sorted, though one of his staff has given everything a quick look, just in case. When a firm calls him in, their definition of 'old' can range from 1660 to 1930.

About half of his present day business is concerned with his stamp auctions, the Globe part of the firm, and he finds this fairly tough, as do most stamp auction people today, but the half that comes out of the old sacks is still booming. All the postal history does well and he thinks he might have one of the largest stocks of postal history in the country. He has fifteen thousand covers — can anybody beat that?

Things like old stocks and shares, bank cheques, canal and railway documents and any sort of pictorial ephemera also sell well. Shopkeepers' bills, if they have a nice vignette at the top, are suddenly proving very popular.

In 1975, it was his back giving out or his knees going which worried him. Now, aged thirty-two, with two children and responsible for his own firm, it's his brain and his eyes which take a battering. His cross in life is now the dreaded VAT man. His business consists of small bits of paper, and each bit, even though most are worth only a couple of pounds, means another bit of paper.

Literary Note: for those of you how have not yet rushed and bought my biography of William Wordsworth. The only job which Wordsworth ever had has a nice connection with what happened in Carlisle some 127 years after his death. He was Distributor of Stamps for Westmorland . . .

Stamp collectors do it between album leaves.

T hey all laughed when I put my stamps in frames and put them on the bathroom and lavatory walls, just as they laughed when Columbus discovered gravity and Archimedes said the world was round. That's the sort of stupid people there are in this house. Laugh at anything they don't understand. We innovators. Go on, scoff, see if I care.

Today a seven-man film crew arrived at our house, or should I say a seven-person crew as the director and the production manager were ladies, still are, at least when they left here. None of your rubbish. The lady in charge was called Sarah and is an award-winning documentary director and the cameraman was called Arthur and he was on the last Bond film. There you are.

I knew the world would see sense in the end and beat a path to our front door, what a shame I didn't mend the gate, and the paintwork's terrible and the dustbins hadn't been emptied, not that any of that matters. What had they come for, this film crew? Why, to make a film about my stamps. That's what.

No you can't be in my film, I told the family. Get back in your cages. You didn't want to look at my lovely stamps yesterday but oh yes, now the band begins to play, it's come on Mr Atkins, do let us see your Penny Reds, have you *really* reconstructed a whole sheet, how marvellous. I know your sort. I'm the star. There are no extras required. Thank you. Don't ring us we certainly won't ring you.

It's a film being made for the Post Office and I take back at once all the rotten things I've ever said about them, such clever people, and they've hired this independent film company to make a twenty minute film which will go out on the circuits, yes, along with the big picture, telling the universe about the wonderful world of stamps. Why did they ask me to be in it? What cheek. How dare you ask such a question.

Actually, I'm not quite sure. Perhaps someone had told them I keep all my collections in frames, displayed on the walls. Or they read about it in *Stamp & Postal History News*. Quite literate, some of these Post Office johnnies. You wouldn't want your daughter to marry them, but I don't mind them coming to the door every morning, back door of course. I keep the front for film crews. Over here, look, this is my good side, forget the stupid stamps, sorry, I mean my treasures, my forehead isn't shining, is it, and you won't let the world see my bald spot.

My mother happens to be staying with us at the moment. I had told all the family what was going to happen today, but they laughed, just another of Hunt's pathetic jokes. Then my mother went into the bathroom and there were three huge blokes *standing* in the bath with enough lights to illuminate Blackpool while a sound crew was crouching on the floor. Don't ask me why they needed sound to get a good shot of my railway stamps. I can hear the steam when I look at them but I don't expect everyone to be so smart. They obviously wanted to do the bathroom shot in sink. Ho ho. Technical joke, don't bother to work it out. We film buffs.

But why me, I asked the director after she'd spent an hour getting the reflection of me looking at my Victorian covers, the ones with our family's initials on, and describing each one. Very hard, looking and talking. They should have got President Ford, but they wanted a younger image.

The film is supposed to show that it's not just kids who

collect stamps, or old fogies in their dotage, but people of all ages with busy, exciting lives, just like you and me. They couldn't get you, as you were far too busy, and probably too over-excited, so they got me. I don't go many places these days.

What we're trying to make clear, she said, is that stamp collectors are not sissies. Hold on, I said, I'll get my football boots.

It sounds a very commendable idea. Anything to help the cause. Stamps do need a bit of glamorous publicity. I'm sure you'll all do your bit when it comes to your local Odeon. I don't know when, possibly in the autumn, but do look out for it. And if I catch you going out for a quick drink on a stick just when it's me and my Penny Reds I'll never speak to you again . . .

The world's first postal services started in China around 4000 BC and in Egypt around 3000 BC. They were used mainly by court officials.

Some very interesting facts supplied by the Post Office

Our wonderful Post Office today runs a fleet of 28,000 motor vehicles — from battery-powered pushcarts to 32-tonne Leyland roadtrains. It also has a stock of 30,000 bicycles. Altogether the postal vehicle fleet covers 317 million miles a year.

On an average day, the Post Office collects more than 37 million letters from 100,000 post office boxes, handles more than 600,000 parcels and delivers to any of 22 million addresses.

The average life of a postman's uniform is two years.

Despite elaborate experiments, carrying mail by rocket has never really got off the ground. Ho ho.

A German scientist called Herr Gerhard Zucker launched the first mail rocket in Britain across the Sussex Downs on June 6, 1934. A mailbag containing 3,000 letters came safely down to earth by parachute, but Herr Zucker was nearly killed by the force of the launch explosion. Undeterred, he tried again. This time the actual rocket exploded, scattering thousands of letters far and wide. He finally gave up his experiments when a test across the Solent from the Isle of Wight to the mainland again went wrong. The rocket was blown off course and the mail dropped in Pennington Marshes.

Cats have been on the official payroll of the Post Office for more than a century. Their job is to keep mice from nibbling the mail. Local postmasters have authority to pay up to £1 per week on pet food for the Post Office mousers. Mice work, if you can get it.

Writer Anthony Trollope will be remembered not just for his books but as the man responsible for the introduction of pillar-boxes in the UK. As a surveyor's clerk with the Post Office the young Trollope was responsible for the siting of pillar-boxes in St Helier, Jersey in 1852. The scheme was quickly extended to the mainland. The oldest pillar-box on the British mainland still in use is at Barnes Cross, Holwell, Bishop's Caundle, Dorset and dates from 1853. Inventing the pillar-box did Trollope's career no harm at all. He went on to become Postmaster General.

In 1874 the Post Office hit on the idea of painting pillar-boxes red. Previously the boxes had been green and were considered dingy. The first pillar-boxes to be experimentally painted red were in Trafalgar Square and Pall Mall. Very soon red became the standard colour throughout London. Within ten years this had spread across the UK and all pillar-boxes were red. Next week, why Tories are painted blue.

There are more than 22,000 post offices in the UK and they come in all shapes and sizes. There has been considerable debate about the smallest post office in Britain. Among the contenders for this title is the post office on the island of Foula, Scotland which is reportedly so small it can hold just one customer at a time. Then there is the post office at Liniero, Isle of Skye which is a cupboard under the stairs at the postmaster's house.

One in ten letters is incorrectly addressed, providing a major headache for Britain's postmen and sorting office staff. As a result of clever detection work, however, 80 per cent of these wrongly addressed letters and parcels arrive at their correct destination. For example, an envelope with just the word 'Arijaba' on it was safely delivered — to Harwich Harbour. And one to 'Claque de Nancy' was sent to Clacton-on-Sea.

Be warned. This is sexist. Everything I am about to say will doubtless be taken up and used against me in evidence as proof of utter prejudice not to mention discrimination. But all I can say, your honour, is that I couldn't help it. I just can't find any theories or explanations which are not sexist to explain the greatest phenomenon in philately: why are there so very few women collectors?

There's nothing basically divisive about stamps, nothing to separate people interested in stamps, one way or the other. You can be big, small, black, white, thin, fat, North, South, up, down, support Spurs or Arsenal, Celtic or Rangers, and yet still be a stamp collector. And as for sexual differences, can you think of anything more utterly sexless in the whole world than stamps?

Let me think. Rod Stewart, he's pretty sexless, Glenda Jackson, she's another, Edward Heath definitely, but apart from them, stamps are some of the few objects in this wicked world which are without any nudge nudge connotations. Freud could see sex everywhere but even he would be hard pressed to dig out any deep and hidden symbolism in philately. 'Sticking them in', well, he might make something out of that phrase, but it would have needed a hard day on the couch to have to stoop so low and vulgar.

According to an in-depth investigation I have just done, and using both fingers to count up the results, I have come to the conclusion that only one per cent of stamp collectors are female. I went down to Covent Garden and entered the London International Stamp Centre, oh spare no expense in this research, and walked around, looking for women. Not a titter, not a petticoat in sight. I asked one of the stall holders, Malcolm Sprei, of M & S Stamps, how many women he had, purely in the way of business of course, and he said on his mail order side he sent out two thousand catalogues and only about ten were to women.

'I think it's because men at home have more leisure,' he said. 'Women are too busy, too involved with the house and family for such hobbies.'

Now, I take *that* as an offensive, sexist remark, and I hope all men will agree. I knock myself out in this house. I don't have any leisure, certainly not. Of his ten lady customers, two in fact buy for their husbands — one because her husband is in hospital and the other because she likes buying her husband presents. In either case, so Sprei said, he always exchanges if the husbands already have the stamps. So, that leaves him with only eight out of two thousand who are serious collectors.

I then talked to Barry Fitzgerald at Embassy stamps and he estimated he had no more than one per cent women amongst his customers. 'It takes great study and love of detail to collect stamps. That's why it appeals mainly to men. It also explains why there are more businessmen than businesswomen and why men are better drivers.

'Women like *visible* things, so they collect porcelain or antiques, paintings or dolls, which they can display for everyone to see, and fuss over and keep tidy. Men like things they can do quietly on their own.

'Mind you, I'd love to have more women customers — and I'd like to see more women in the stamp world generally. What I'd really like is for dealers to have more dolly birds working for them. That would make my private life much more fun . . . '

Thank you, Barry, we'll be in touch, unless you get a feminist brick through your window first. Suddenly, I spotted two ladies and I immediately accosted them. It was a mother and daughter and the daughter was buying a picture postcard of the Pope, with a Cardiff postmark on it. She said she collects picture postcards of famous people and stamps to do with Churchill or Kennedy. Her mother said she used to collect stamps, but passed them all on to her daughter. She got her interest in stamps from her father. Her husband has no interest in stamps, or postcards or any collecting hobby.

It appears that on the thematic side there are probably quite a few women collectors, though still very much in the minority. As thematics continue to grow, perhaps we'll have more women amongst us. I've also noticed recently that many Mums do a bit of stamp buying, going on Saturday mornings to their local stamp shop with their children.

On the whole, though, stamps seem to be a male preserve.

Now a joke from the racing world: do stamp collectors' wives also get covered on the first day?

Have you got any other explanations, or any facts and figures? Or any dolly birds for Barry? Coming shortly, legal actions willing, I hope to talk to some lady dealers, if I can find any, and ask them what they think about the lack of women in stamps.

Stamp collectors do it in gutters.

I rashly promised that I would bring you, warm on a plate, almost fresh from the oven, some more half-baked theories about Women in Stamps. At least the lack of Women in Stamps. I will now attempt for my next feat, or should it be meet-her, to talk to a few lady dealers.

The trouble I've had, don't ask me. Where are they all? I looked through the pages of *Stamp & Postal History News*, trific publication, really good, you should buy it, stead of nicking someone else's copy, hoping to see some ladies advertising their wares, know what I mean. Stanley, that's not a girl's name, nor is Robson Lowe I don't think, and Argyll Etkin is giving nothing away, nor is Cavendish or Harmer. Urch Harris sounds like an expletive. There were quite a few neutered firms hiding behind sets of initials, but not a feminine Christian name in sight.

Then I remembered that the Hampstead Stamp Shop, where I used to waste away my middle age, seemed to be run by a lady, Margaret Kon, but they have now closed, alas. I tracked her down to a P.O. Box No — 904 W9 1PG. How unglamorous after that smart address in Hampstead. She's now postal dealing and doing quite well. I said I want some facts, ma'am, just the facts. Who's in charge round here, I rasped out the words on the telephone, one foot in the door of the E–K Directory. We investigators use every modern device.

I was worried that she would turn out to be just another sidekick, junior partner, stuck on the notepaper to look businesslike. There are quite a few husband and wife teams out there, with the wife making up the numbers, doing the draggy jobs, in the hope that one day a killing will be made and as a director, all the huge profits can then be kept in the family. Some hope. But all little dealers live in hope.

No, she said, I am the dealer, I'm in charge. It all began twelve years ago when the Salvation Army phosphors started shooting up the price and she decided to do a bit of spare time dealing. When her husband Eddie lost his job in the motor trade, she took up dealing full-time, with her husband helping, to support her family. 'I think it's great when the woman is the breadwinner. I came in at the right time. Now I think it's very hard for anyone to get in, male or female.

'Traditionally, ninety-nine per cent of the stamp business has been male. I collected as a little girl in Malaya, but I was made to feel it was a boy's hobby. As a dealer, I have felt hostility at times. They think as a woman you don't know much. I do get mad when the male chauvinist pigs belittle women. I tell them oh well, I'll just have to learn from male chauvinist pigs like you . . .

'When I'm in a shop, browsing, I know the dealer will think I'm not a serious collector, because I'm a woman. My name is on the letterhead of my firm, but all the letters still come addressed: "Dear Sir" . . .'

I then rang a lady called Carol Higdon in Newton Abbot, Devon, having recalled seeing her name on some rather nice notepaper when I'd bought stuff from Longmead Philatelics. (They use the Mulready design, as do the Globe people in Carlisle, and probably others do as well, don't tell me.)

She said theirs was a joint husband and wife partnership, though she had been a collector before her husband Richard had taken it up. They too have very few women collectors. 'Women haven't got the time. You have to sit down with your stamps. You can't just jump up and attend to something else every moment, the way women have to do.' As a dealer, though, she had felt no prejudice or discrimination.

'Men have always been the great stamp people,' said her husband. 'Look at the famous collectors. All of them are men. The great forgers, they were men. All the great nutters were men. I don't know the reasons why. You would need a psychologist to explain.'

P.S. If there are any psychologists out there who also happen to be stamp collectors, please get in touch, in a plain envelope. I will do all I can to help. Thanks.

A nother season, another reason, for making Whoopee. Tra la. As if you ever need seasons or reasons for making Whoopee. But stamps are different. There is of course no reason whatsoever for collecting stamps, as we all know that it is a madness which cannot be explained. But is there a season for stamps?

I ask this question to myself, as I'm the only one listening, and unlike the jesting Pilate I am prepared to stay for an answer. I just happen to be sitting here looking at a huge pile of stuff which I have collected over the last few months, all fantastically precious to me, things I'd set my heart on, if only I could get them, oh please let my incredibly low bid at that auction be the winner, let no one turn up at that little sale in the back of beyond, and oh God fingers crossed that they're all dumdums and don't know what they're selling. You have to have fantasies, if you're a stamp collector.

But behold and lo, I have accumulated quite a few goodies for my various collections in recent weeks. Yet I have done nothing with them. What has happened to me? If they were so important, why have I just left them lying there in that old shoe box?

Look at those beautiful Wembleys, bought at Robson Lowe in Bournemouth back in April, yet they're still in the registered envelope. I lay awake, worrying about them, would I have to mortgage the house, would we have to live on bread and water, should I leave the country or put Not Known, Return to Sender on the envelope when they arrived?

And those trific sheets of 1966 World Cup stamps, the GB ones with the sexy legs, which I bought with such excitement at South Eastern Auctions, what have I done with them? Nothing. I was going to frame them and put them in the lavatory, as is my wont, and amuse all our visitors during the 1982 World Cup. Missed it completely. Might as well wait now till 1986.

Over here, there's a packet from James of Norwich, full of Lake District postcards with some postal history markings I'd long been searching for. And what did I do when I got them? *Rien. Nada.* Then here's some vital missing stamps for my reconstructions of 1841 Tuppenny Blues which I got from Phillips, all waiting to be given their pride of place. Unseen, unloved, unopened.

I don't worry too much about that pile of unopened presentation packs sent from the Post Office in Edinburgh. I'm

"I'm what you might call an Under Cover Agent ! "

already fed up with them. The sizes keep on changing, there are just so many, where can I file them without spending even more money? I think when my present subscription comes to an end I'll stop them. I buy them out of charity, to help the post office. And are they grateful? Certainly not. It will be cheaper in future just to buy any new commemoratives I happen to like, which is getting rarer anyway, from our local post office.

I know what my wife will say should I moan to her. 'More money than sense.' Luckily, I keep such thoughts to myself, apart from sharing it with you out there, and you over there, all fellow amateur collectors who, I'm sure will understand and who also keep it a state secret how much money leaves the house every month in search of some more very wonderful stamps.

Stamps must be a winter pastime, that's it. We need the long dark nights to curl up with a good album, an exciting pair of tweezers and a box of Penny Black Magic. Philatelists are lonely figures, hiding away, doing unmentionable things to themselves in the privacy of their rooms, lost in their own little worlds, so naturally they prefer the winter time. These long summer light nights. How can I get down to my collections? Who knows what Toms might be Peeping.

There are also so many rival attractions and activities in the summer, at least in my little life. My summer hols are coming up, which will mean a break from that brain power and eye power I put into trying to decipher those cheap nasty dupli-cated catalogues produced on kitchen tables where you need a magnifying glass to see the pages, never mind work out the small print.

Even more important, because I am about to go away, I have to get ahead. We self-employed book writers, living at home on our wits, we have to keep working all the time. It means work-ing *doubly* hard before a holiday, just to keep up. It's okay for you salaried slaves, paid holidays and all that. Lucky.

So, that explains it. I am not neglecting my treasures. It's simply that I suddenly have too many other things to do. Work, the curse of the stamp-collecting classes.

Did you know that stamps go dead, but dead, cold as a deceased parrot, every year in Australia from Christmas till the end of January? Nobody wants to know. You can hardly give them away, that's if you could find any stamp collectors out and about and walking straight and narrow. This is what stamp retailers say, Down Under.

Oh, just one of the many tit bits I have picked up in a mammoth investigation I am conducting into whether there is a season in stamps. I know that I personally have little time or interest to mess around with my stamps in the summer months, but I was wondering what the experts out there think. Not just Down There. I mean out there, in the wonderful world of British stamp dealing, not a million miles from the jolly old Strand.

Robson Lowe have sales in London and Bournemouth, all the year round, and maintain that auction business comes in a steady flow, with no seasonable variation. In Bournemouth, they often get slightly higher attendances in the summer, for sales and exhibitions, as dealers just happen to arrange their summer holidays to take a few days at sunny Bournemouth.

"Fifty million Christmas stamps please!"

They're not stupid, some of these dealers, despite what you might think from their expressions when you go in and ask if they've got any cheap stuff, you know, where's the bargain box? I often think I'm speaking in a foreign language, judging by the look on their faces.

'If you have good things to auction,' said Peter Collins of Robson Lowe, 'then the season doesn't matter. People will still come and buy. We are international auctioneers anyway, so things even up throughout a whole year. We had a huge success with our New Guinea sale in July, despite it being the so-called holiday season, but it contained great material.'

It's the same with little local stamp activities. I went to a local stamp club on the night that England played Spain to stay in the World Cup. I thought no one would turn up. But it was packed. It was a talk on Zeppelins, which of course is a fascinating subject, and that brought people in.

As for the retailers, most London stamp shops seem to do particularly well in the summer, thanks to all the visitors. From Brighton to the Lake District, stamp shops in holiday places also seem pretty crowded at this time of the year. I'm not sure they're buying much, but there's a lot of hanging around, especially if it's raining.

Stanley Gibbons say that on their shop side they have two definite peaks every year. August is always a bumper month, with overseas visitors heading for the heart of the stamp empire, and non-London Brits giving themselves their once-a-year chance to see Gibbons in the flesh. The other big month is November, which is quite surprising. Firstly, it's because collectors have spent October looking at their albums again, after the summer break, wondering what to buy next to fill in the gaps. Secondly, it's the beginning of the Christmas season, with people buying presents.

On their rare stamp side, the position is completely different. The peak is in September and it keeps up fairly well till March, then it falls gradually, with July and August being the pits. These are all generalisations, although well-marked. Hardened addicts, of all sorts, will buy at any time.

So it looks as if some of the retail trade at least thinks this summer is not a bad time for them, thank you very much. This year, I think they have one person in particular to thank. Step forward Lady Di, the patron saint of the stamp trade. What would they have done without her. Imagine organising her birthday so it fell in the middle of the summer. How thoughtful of her.

Personally, I don't want to see another special offer for special Royal Princess Stamps from some special lump of rock in a special ocean I've never heard of. You can't get moving for them. It's like muzak is for people not interested in music and sliced bread is for people not interested in bread. Royal Birthday stamps are for people not interested in stamps.

I'm looking forward to my holidays in Portugal next week. I know a little shop in Lagos where I always poke around the old postcards, hoping for some treasures. If I find he's selling stuff with the same old photographs of Lady Di's face on, yet more labels wishing her a Happy Birthday, I will probably scream. Then next year I'll go to Australia instead. Probably in January . . .

'SAVE FUEL — USE YOUR YELLOW PAGES.' That's what the Post Office slogan said. They of course have got money to burn . . .

My letter life has increased tremendously since I took up stamps again just three years ago. I now get rubbish by every post. I hope you always fill your name in on those forms from dealers offering you their catalogues for free. I always do. Makes one feel sort of important. Proof of existence. Then when they ask you take out a subscription for next year, sob sob, or they will go bust and be on bread and gruel and really they can't afford it and they are trying terribly hard to bring you bargains, bargains, then I ignore them and fill in another coupon. Heh ho. Life is good.

Today, I had three good things in the post, apart from all the junk. It takes hours these days, opening my post.

I tear off every stamp, first or second class, tatty or otherwise. At one time I kept only the high values, or commemoratives or foreign, but now I devour every scrap. Yes, dear, I know. I'm going to clear up that mess. Just give me a moment. God's truth, I'm not a machine. Yes, those bits of paper are precious. I'm going to leave them in that water and then pull them apart, all neat and tidy, but just give me time.

I did a batch the other day, leaving them in the bathroom sink, after I'd shaved. Then I forget about them. That evening I had to get out the plunger as they had fouled up the whole system with gunge.

The first interesting thing in the post was a catalogue from Robson Lowe for a sale of GB stuff belonging to some terribly famous collector called J. O. Griffiths.

Mainly Penny Blax and Tuppenny Blooz, by the look of the pictures. Ye Gods. I felt like giving up at once. How can I ever compete. I had to avert my eyes as if they were *hard-pore corn. Disgusting. Should not be allowed. I won't be going to the sale, which anyway is in Zurich, nor making any bids, have you seen the prices? But in the long winter nights ahead when I'm feeling Robson Lowe I'll take out the catalogue and ogle the photographs.

Then there was a letter from Mrs Irene Lawford, now she is famous, of the Philatelic Music Circle, who proceeded to wrap me over the knuckles with her Baton (joke, gerrit, that's the name of her organ). You may recall I wrote something about women not being collectors. I cannot remember my precise words. I've better things to do than read this sort of rubbish. Oh yes, she says here, it's not true, as I alleged, that there are only a few women on the thematic side. In the Philatelic Music Circle, half the members are women. So there, Hunt. I sit corrected. Very sorry, Irene, or can I call you Ms?

As for my third letter, well, I don't know where to hide my blushes. I've been informed that the British Philatelic Federation has awarded me a prize. I immediately rushed

---

*hard-pore corn is the stuff that is smuggled in through Gatport Airwick.

round the house shouting yaroo, chaps, listen to this, none of yous lot has ever won a prize in your rotten lives, but look at this, Philatelic Journalist of the Year, perhaps the Century, yes me, little old me.

I've been writing books and journalism for twenty years now, man and superman, turning out twenty books and two million words, and all this time I've never won nuffink. I think in 1969 I did get £10 on the Premium Bonds, what a day that was, but let's not rest on old laurels, or was it £5, I can't remember.

My wife looked at the letter carefully. It was not exactly as I had led myself to believe. It turns out to be a prize for being the best-read writer in *Stamp & Postal History News*. She was very scornful. Bloody hell, winning something organised by that. I bet it was a fiddle. You're just jealous, I said.

You might remember the competition. All you clever readers out there had to vote for the things you like best in *Stamp & Postal History News*. (When I said dumdum, I was just choking. You know that. Ha ha.) Guess who came out top. Yup. Autographs later.

I was invited down to a big banquet in Southampton but alas I couldn't make it. Pressure of work. I've got all these envelopes to open and stamps to unstick, haven't I? But I still get my award. Wait for it. Take it easy. Fifty pounds! Life is even gooder.

"It was a re-gumming factory but the fumes went to his head."

I am sitting here looking at a stamp I have on approval. First I say: 'I will', then I say: 'Don't be daft, Hunt, you certainly will not'. On the other hand, I might regret it, if perhaps another example doesn't come my way for years. On the third hand, I will certainly regret it if next week I find a nicer example at a cheaper price. Oh God, if only I'd stuck to fretwork. None of this would have happened.

It's almost the final missing link in my collection of Victorian stamps. I'm talking about GB, of course. Are there any others? My very handsome Windsor album, hand-tooled in something made of green, will then be complete, if I buy this one, except for a QV £5 stamp which I won't worry about too much, not for the next few years. At the price I'll have to pay for one of those, who needs worries.

The one I'm looking at is the first pound, the square one of 1867, and I've been searching for one for over a year now. In the ancient and modern hymn book, the SG number is 129, though this particular example is SG 132, cos of the watermark. It looks horrible, really nasty. You can't see the rotten old Queen's head for the cancellation. I must be out of my tiny mind and if my wife comes into the room now, while I'm staring at this scruffy scrap, and finds that I'm thinking of paying £90 for it, she'll have a seizure.

Perhaps I better say no. It really is obscene. Think of all the starving Chinese I could buy for that price. When I started my GB collection, just three years ago, I vowed never to pay more than £10 for any stamp. Ah, such innocence.

However, pause, thinking hard, pause, it is remarkably cheap. A good example, in prime condition, could knock you back almost £2,000. 'Cleverly repaired top corner tip,' so it said in the Lamonby and Allen catalogue. That never bothers me, so I rang them straight away in Portsmouth, at mid-morning, peak time, I must be made of money, and they kindly sent it, along with another which I'm definitely buying, for me to look at. Yes, there probably is a slight repair, but who cares about that. The real worry is the nasty inky cancellation. 'Rather heavy' so they said. I think the postman must have climbed up and jumped on it.

What it brings into question is my whole philosophy of stamp collecting. For three years now, I have blithely gone ahead buying bad stamps. I still will buy bad stamps. In fact I love bad stamps. King of the Space Fillers, that's me. I ignore all these boring experts who advise me otherwise. If I like it, and it passes my very low acceptance standard, then it's straight in the album, no messing. First rule, if it's cheap, gerrit. It's like wine. My favourite vintage is £1.75 a bottle. That was a very good year, not as good as £1.65, but I'll still drink it, cheers.

This lady expert in Gibbons told me two years ago, when I happened to flash a Penny Black I'd got for £15, what a bargain already, okay it looked as if the dog had had it for breakfast, but what do you expect for £15, that in a year I would become dissatisfied with it and would want a better example. I'm still happy, thank you, very pleased I didn't buy a £150 one with full margins and no bites out of it. I don't mind repairs, no gum, no margins, creases, tears, bits out of the side and it can be thin enough to spit through, just as long as the design is still there and you can see what it is.

I'm not in stamps for investment. I'd be buying property if I wanted to make money, not boring old stamps. I'm in stamps for fun. Yes, I know, don't tell me, that my rubbish stamps will hardly increase in value in the future, if at all. See if I care. Yes, I do know that I should have put all the money into one good stamp and not bought these hundreds of tatty copies. No dealer will ever want these. My only hope would be another fool like me.

There's something so desiccated and dreary and dull about these experts who fuss over all the draggy minor details. I've fallen into that trap with my Wembley collection, which is a specialised thing, but in my general GB album, I'm determined to stay superficial. Bad is beautiful.

But there's bad and bad. So far, even with my other high values, none of them has been as filthy as this. Technically, it's in very good condition, for its price. It has those pin prick holes, perfins, I think they are called, which explains its cheapness, but they don't worry me. It's just that horrible black splodge on her conk. For a cleaner one, I'll probably have to pay more like £200. But when will I ever see one of those?

That empty space on page 23 is haunting me. Perhaps I'll put it in now, try it out for sighs. Not a bad little fit. Hmm. Okay then, Mr Lamonby and Mr Allen, the money's in the post, but not a word to Bessie . . .

Philatelists do it in their armchairs.

S ome time ago I was chuntering on about women in stamps, or the lack of them, wondering why there are so few lady collectors. I said, as a joke, that it would take a psychologist to explain the reasons, if only I could find a psychologist who also happens to be a stamp collector.

Guess what. Oh, you've guessed. Yup, a real live stamp collector who also happens to be a psychologist who also happens to be a woman has written to me. What a specimen. I felt like getting out my butterfly net and capturing her, pinning her down in a jumbo-sized Hawid mount and sticking her in my biggest album. She would be able to breath okay. Through the perforations. Ho ho.

Instead, I got out my green eyeshade and my reporter's notebook and asked her a few impertinent questions, such as how old are you? I don't know why I still do that. It's my early training on the *Manchester Evening Chronicle*. No matter if there were bodies all over the ground, you had firstly to get their names and ages then find out which ones lived in Wigan or Eccles so that we could get them in the early editions.

I did get her name, which is Gloria McAdam of Dewsbury in Yorkshire, but not her age. 'If I say as old as Zsa Zsa Gabor when she was twenty-nine, I don't think I'm far out.' Failed again. But she sounds young, with a young son called Benjy, and it was he who started her off on the stamp trail six years ago.

'It was an attempt to keep him from demolishing the hall with a football. I bought him a cheap stamp album, a few stamps and a jar of Copydex carpet adhesive. The adhesive and his interest ran out and I took over.'

She now specialises in Africa, plus Scottish postal history and other bits and pieces. 'In truth I haven't really started collecting yet. I've just been hoarding for the past five years. I suspect I enjoy the reference books more than the collectables. One day I hope to find time to specialise in the postal history of British Africa.'

She has, however, found time to try to resell some of the spare junk, I mean treasures, she has accumulated on the way. Her experience of this sounds just like mine, and I'm sure hundreds of others. What fools we all are.

'During the holidays, I stood at one or two stamp fairs

hoping to offload sacks of stuff purchased in moments of weakness. The customers didn't want it any more than I did, and I had to hump it all back home again.'

Anyway, Gloria, let's have the benefit of all that post-grad work you've done in experimental psychology and tell us why we all collect?

'Stamp collecting is a very personal thing and there are probably as many reasons for collecting as there are collectors. Take me, for example. My first collection, Imperial Russia, all started because I had a soft spot for the Tsar. Then when I moved into my religious period I started collecting Vatican. One psychologist has explained collecting as a form of insecurity — a need for possessions which will reflect the individual's personality. It could be a hoarding instinct in that we're all squirrels at heart. I've been told that squirrels forget where they put things. This is particularly so in my case...'

And what about women, why are they so thin on the ground? 'I'm not sure there are any fewer women in stamps than there are in the majority of hobbies and sports which have traditionally been male-dominated. There are pastimes which are considered specifically feminine in which very few men indulge. Perhaps there's a fear of appearing odd, mannish, womanish, whatever. We are very conditioned into our respective sex roles and the majority of people feel most comfortable in the company of their own sex.

'I spend my life, at home and at work, surrounded by men. I'm not complaining. But I do sometimes wonder why there are so few men interested in flower arranging...'

Thanks, Gloria. Now who's next on the line? I'd like to hear from any brain surgeons who collect Wembley stamps, to see if I need my head examining, and any computer programmer who collects Penny Blacks who will tell me why it is that out of 68,000,000 printed all mine are in shreds.

Stamp collectors do it collectively.

I'm a bit worried about the image of we or should it be us stamp collectors. Either road up, we seem to be considered by the general public to be a fairly miserable lot. You know and I know that collecting stamps is a fun-filled pastime, a hobby so exciting that we often have to sit alone in a dark room to cool down, an occupation so dangerous that we often go around in gutter pairs. But does the rest of the world know all this or even care? Do they heckers.

Dull, dreary and dopey, not to mention stupid, waste of time, draggy, how can you do it, how old are you, haven't you anything better to do with your middle age, why don't you grow up, do something useful for once, get yourself a worthwhile hobby, and so on, and that's just a random sample of the opinions in this house, over here, where I'm sitting. You could probably find similar comments in your own home, not all of them printable. Oh, I know, I have tried. I point out how I'm helping to ease the unemployment situation. But for me, hundreds of stamp dealers would be on the streets, throwing themselves out of the upstairs window of Stanley Gibbons, that big plate glass one, what a lovely way to go.

What has really upset me is Bobby Robson. You know, the manager of the England football team, which is a joke for a start, call that a team, my Sunday morning Dads' team could hammer them. I have before me the *Guardian* in which Robson is quoted as saying something so disgusting that I hope by now the British Philatelic Federation has been on the blower to Lord Goodman. He was apparently being asked how the quality of the country's schoolboy footballers could be improved and he replied by saying that for a start they should not be wasting their time 'climbing trees and collecting stamps'. Now, the National Association of Tree-Climbers can well look after themselves, and they have branches in high places, but who has sprung to the defence of us or is it we stamp collectors? Diabolical liberty, if you ask me. What a cheek. Saatchi and Saatchi, where are you now, now that we need you?

'The World's Greatest Hobby.' Yes, I suppose that slogan does trundle through a million letter boxes every day, but it doesn't grab you, does it? Not exactly sexy, or finger-licking good, or funny, or silly, or even socio-economically arresting.

Just blank and bland. Doesn't offend anyone, unless it's coin collectors.

So, just to help all my comrades along, my fellow travellers in philately, I would like to make a few suggestions. I don't expect dealers to do much. They're all injured at the moment, fallen off their wallets. It is up to the ordinary collectors to do their bit for England and St George, plus the Falklands, all the Crown Agent Territories, even Turks and Caicos, Tuvalu, Tristan da Cunha and those lumps of uninhabited rocks everywhere which I usually refuse to mention, but at such a time, it's backs to the wall, true grit, everyone must help.

I want you to think of a slogan which will excite the nation about the wonderful world of stamp collecting. Most of all, I think it should be neat enough to be used as a little sticker to put in the back of our car windows. Why should all those other boring activities have all the fun and all the bad jokes.

'Windsurfers do it standing up.' You must have seen that one in the back of a clapped-out old Cortina. 'Hang gliders do it upside down.' 'Young farmers do it in green wellies.' 'Photographers do it in the dark.' You must have seen all of those.

I even noticed one in the *Bookseller* this week, the trade magazine of the publishing world. 'Publishers do it by the book.' Someone somewhere is printing and selling all these little stickers, and other idiots are buying them. But have you spotted one yet about stamp collecting? There you are. Nobody cares about we.

I've been trying hard to think of a good one. 'Stamp Collectors do it on their own.' Hmm, it might be true, but those are not the connotations we want to encourage, though it has to be a little bit saucy, otherwise those Cortina drivers won't want to know. And if it is saucy enough, we could make the *Sun*.

'Philately gets you everywhere.' Not bad, Hunt, quite clever, but it hasn't enough, how shall I put it, zip.

'Stamp collectors always stick it in.' No, too rude. Anyway the Hawid people would complain, and the Hagner people. We'll never get the Volvo drivers with that one.

'Stamp collectors stick together.' Heh, that's not bad. Hands up for that one?

On reflection, just to get us started — and I hope you'll send in *your* suggestions for a saucy slogan — my best favourite so far is this one. 'Stamp collectors do it with tweezers.' It's just so silly, it could catch on.

The letter-sorting manager at Peterborough Post Office is called Mr Missin.

I have a moral dilemma. You didn't think we amateur faint-hearted, lily-livered stamp collectors experienced such a problem; Ho yus. Many is the time I have regretted the hours I have put in with my albums, my shoe boxes, my tatty envelopes when I know I should have been out there fighting in the front line for my wife and family, earning enough bread to keep the Vatman from the door instead of frittering my life away. What good, after all, are fritters when the day of reckoning comes?

Then how oft have I sinned when I have crept into the house, my guilty secret in a plain cover, furtively hiding those give-away initials, the dreaded SG and stepped stealthily up the stairs to my little room and quickly got out a rubber and erased those tell-tale figures, carefully changing £10 to £1 so that the world, and my wife, will never find out what I have done? Forgive me.

And yet, I have come to live with such errors and weaknesses. Life goes on. We bend and twist, alter our standards, confess and go on, and really Hunt I wish you would go on as this introduction is out of all proportion. Here goes then. I am about to confess all.

I have been offered a handsome amount of money to do a half-hour radio programme extolling the virtues of the

Commonwealth Collection. You must have heard about it. The advertisements have been everywhere throughout the stamp press and in the colour magazines. A limited amount of special albums are being issued for Commonwealth Day, March 14, containing all the special Commonwealth stamps. A snip — at only £145.

There you are, did I sneer in that last paragraph? Certainly not. I just stated the facts. It's up to you, friends, to decide whether it's a load of old nonsense, taking money off dumdums who know no better. I gather the face value of the stamps is around £60, but of course with the album you are getting gilt-edged elegance and special parchment paper, so it says in the hand-tooled prose of the advertisements. Who am I to knock such a truly wonderful and unprecedented historic souvenir?

All week I have agonised. Should I take the money and run? After all, it is for a worthy cause, so it says, helping something called the Commonwealth Fund for Technical Co-operation. And Her Gracious Majesty has written a foreword. She doesn't go around writing forewords or even backwords in any old place, does she? (And I should hope not. There are enough of us trying to earn an honest living shifting words without Her coming into the business as well. I bet she's not in the NUJ or the Writer's Guild. But we needn't go into all that.)

The trouble is I feel, deep down in my bones, that all these commemorative stamps, which all countries these days produce, all of the time, are just labels. Okay, so they make a vital income for each country. They amuse the kids. They keep the Post Office's philatelic counter workers off the streets. But count me out. I have this rule, which I'm sure I've told you about, that I don't collect things that have been produced to be collected. Well done, Hunt. What a purist.

But hold on, clever clogs. Don't be so virtuous. Did you not mention only the other day in this very column that you paid a large sum of money for a Wembley Exhibition First Day Cover? If you are being strictly principled, are not all first day covers souvenirs, created simply to be collected? Get out of that, Hunt.

Yes, well. I'm just a humble writer. Don't confuse me with all this Aristotle stuff. Anyway, rules are meant to be broken. That's what my third form teacher used to say. Wembley was a very long time ago and the comparison is not strictly fair. You could get those First Day postmarks for free, if you posted your letters and cards at the right place at the right time. It's the trade since that has put a price on them. Let's not argue, eh. This is all giving me a headache.

Yes, it's been a heavy week. Every day have I tortured myself, rationalising why I *should* do it, thinking what a lovely new stamp, I mean lovely old stamps, I could buy with the money, then deciding no, don't do it Hunt. Be a man. You could never attack any commemorative issue or limited edition, ever again. So what did I do folks? Stand on your head to find out . . .

I turned the offer down.

"Got it! You are looking for a tête-beche pair!"

Stamp collectors wrap it up in a plastic sheath.

I hope I haven't fallen again. I vowed to myself that I would never again be seduced and become victim to some passing fancy. At my age, I should be over all that. And yet it is exactly at my age, forty-six getting on twenty-seven, that people do these silly things on a sudden impulse, completely out of character, captivated by a shapely silhouette or the sight of a pretty head.

I was wandering this morning round some open-air stalls at Camden Town, putting in the hours, putting in the days, with Flora, my ten-year-old daughter. She was looking for jewellery or leg-warmers or ra-ra skirts and other essentials of modern life and I was poking through the odd box of rubbishy postcards, the sort they put in a heap at 5p each and you know quite well that every hanger-about in the Western Hemisphere has already thumbed through them, but, hope springs, the sap also rises. You never know, there might be a first-day Wembley post card lurking amongst the junk which every one else has missed. Some hope.

I kept asking at each stall if they had any stamps but no one had. There is often a bloke selling stamps, just modern commemoratives for the kids, nothing of note, but when time hangs I'm willing to look at anything. He wasn't there today.

Collectors are collectors. They collect collections. It is a disease which knows no bounds. What do *you* collect? To which the paid-up fanatic will always answer very simply, What have you got to get rid of? Most collectors are in the market for almost anything, though they keep a very wary eye on themselves, pretending they are specialists, looking perhaps only for stamps, in fact only *one* sort of stamps, but out of the corner of their eye, through a crack in their mind, they are always willing to consider a little flutter on the side. Not a word to the Good Lady.

On this particularly scruffy stall I happened to see a familiar physiognomy, good old Queen Victoria, smiling away regally at me, giving me the royal eye. This was a much older version, a late middle-aged, nay an elderly Queen. As we stampers know, she appears on all our Victorian stamps in only one design, remaining a young girl right to the end of her reign. I do prefer the older woman these days.

I picked up this coin and admired it, especially its price. Only

10p for a genuine Victorian penny. What a bargain. Coin collectors have all the luck. I suppose the cheapest stamp with the Queen's head on, a Penny Red say, would cost you a minimum of 30p. The cheapest Penny Black, in tatty condition, with no margins, would cost more like £10.

The man on the stall explained that you could collect three sorts of Victorian pennies, all very cheaply, each with a different head of the Queen — as a young girl, with a bun, and as an old woman. So I did. I actually paid £1.25 for all of them, in fine condition. He was a gentle, easy going, un-pushy sort of dealer, prepared to give me a lesson in coin collecting, all for nothing, for just as long as I wanted to chat. I found it all fascinating.

Then I noticed he had some Roman coins. Despite having written a book some years ago about Hadrian's Wall, which of course you have all read, I never actually found myself a Roman coin, though I looked everywhere on my walk. I had not imagined it would be within my purse to *buy* a Roman coin. He had one for sale at only £3.50, a coin clearly showing the head of the Emperor Constantine I, 307–337. He said it could be mine for £3! So I fell. I just could not believe it. An object almost two thousand years old, for only £3. What am I doing in stamps, wasting all my money on these silly bits of modern scrap paper.

I rushed home and went into the garage with Flora. I have had this tin of old pre-decimal pennies lying around for years, all dirty and rusty. The bloke on the stall had told me that if I could find a 1933 penny he would pay me £1,000 for it. Or anything from the 1950s he would also buy, for up to £20 perhaps, depending on the year and condition. We raced through the piles of pennies in a lather. And found nothing. Apparently only six 1933 pennies were minted, though I did not tell Flora that, not till we had exhausted the tin, and ourselves.

I promised her I will buy her a presentation set of all our decimal coins at the post office tomorrow morning. This could be the start of something big, Flora, what a marvellous new hobby for you, Flora, then I realised she had gone off, completely bored. I had been left talking to myself. So I stopped. Just in time. Phew, what an escape.

Where could this day of madness have led to. I have enough to worry about, haven't I? All those Penny Blacks and

Wembleys out there, just waiting for me to snatch them up. How can I possibly go off with another passion? What a faithless person I have become. Like President Carter, I have sinned in my mind.

Right, cold shower now and off to bed. In the morning I'll pretend that today never happened . . .

Stamp collectors do it to help Hunter Davies to fill up space . . .

I've never been a great fan of Bernard Levin. Oh, I know he's clever and fluent and very good on long sentences and even longer paragraphs and it is amazing how he has managed all these years to keep turning it out regularly, polished and smart, with the correct capital letters and commas and parentheses and all that culture thrown in and foreign words and quotes from the greats and oh, now I see why it's so easy to write long sentences. Someone has stolen the full stop on this typewriter. Got it. Phew.

I don't care for his personal obsessions, such as opera. Then there was all that Indian mystical stuff and regenerating the world and that inner awareness tosh. Most of all, I dislike the praise he always gets, the adulation he has acquired, the following he gets. Call it jealousy if you will. Thanks. I'll remember that.

All this has been pure prejudice, of course, secret thoughts I have kept to myself these last few years. I haven't wanted to be out of step, and anyway, what have I really got against him? Nothing, apart from that dreaded English disease which we all seem to suffer from. A desire to knock anyone who gets to the top. Everyone who knows him well says he is terribly nice. A real gent. Lovely feller.

So I have learned to live with my prejudice, and forgive him for being so successful and popular, when I chanced to pick up Sunday's *Observer*. I get it for my staff, of course. The servants do love its Colour Magazine. Mr Levin was reviewing a bio-

"Some people collect stamps - we collect postmen!"

graphy of C. P. Snow. During this review, for no reason whatsoever, except a blatant smear and unprovoked attack, he came out with a remark which I hardly dare repeat.

'He collected honorary degrees the way even sillier men collect stamps.'

Right, lads. I'll take the first spell on the picket line. I want the rest of you to get round to Gray's Inn Road first thing in the morning. Take up your position outside the front door of *The Times*. No bricks through the window till I shout.

I will let the collectors of honorary degrees look after their own campaign. Lord Olivier has hundreds and though he's not well at the moment, no doubt Vanessa Redgrave will march willingly on his behalf. These honorary degree people will probably get all the publicity, as they include the sort of famous faces the cameras love. We stamp collectors are a much quieter bunch, anonymous, gentle folk, retiring and patient, but my word, when our danders are up, when we get pricked do we not bleed. We will show the world what we are made of. We won't take this lying down in the gutter pairs.

Now is the time to rise before our oppressors. I have sinned myself in the past. I admit it. Before I got the call three years ago, and opened up again my childhood albums, I was often guilty of nasty remarks about stamp collectors. I used to dismiss wet people as the sort who did 'fretwork or collected stamps'. There. I have now confessed all. But like all reformed sinners, I am doubly passionate, now that I have been converted and seen the light. Perhaps St Bernard will one day regret all and leave the sordid, media, capitalist world of Fleet Street and retire into a monastery to contemplate his Penny Black plates and count his perforations.

In the meantime, we must all do what we can and help in any way to improve the image of stamp collecting and prevent such nasty sneers and jibes being made at our expense. Which naturally brings me to my slogan for stamps, the best words to go on a car sticker for all stamp collectors to display. Never was there a more vital time to mount our campaign.

I have had some rather rude slogans this week, many of them from Major Ronnie Spafford. He suggests them only to say they are the sort he would not like to see. 'I do it with gum on my back.' Hmm, rather silly I think. 'The mint with the holes round the side.' You could be on to a nice one there, Ronnie, but you'll have to work a bit harder. 'Wrap it up in a plastic sheath.' That should appeal to sixth formers, being their sort of silly joke, or Mr Hawid. 'Unzip your envelope with care.' Vulgar and not even funny. 'Does yours need a magnifying glass?' No comment. 'Have gum, will travel.' That's quite neat, Ronnie. Keep trying.

I have carefully kept all the slogans you have sent, for which many thanks. I'll wait another few weeks for any late-comers, for any other flashes of inspiration you might have. This could be a real break-through in stamps, the turning-point in our public image. Then I plan to parcel them all up and post them to the cleverest man in the Western Hemisphere. B. Levin, of course. He'll know what to do with them...

Stamp collectors love to do it tête-bêche.

I have now got so many I'm thinking of opening a Christmas Cracker factory. For 1984 of course. Too late now for this year and I'm certainly not doing anything to help old 1983. Nasty thing.

I did start to write little thank-you notes to every reader who sent in a suggestion, being well brought up, clean about the house, kind to all charities especially the Post Office which is by far my favourite charity and this year, goodness, I must have contributed thousands to their coffers. But my wrist was aching in the end. Then a drowsy numbness reached my brain and I began to wonder if it was hemlock I had drunk or reading the *Guardian* every morning. So I stopped individual replies. This is to say thanks to everyone.

Colin Wilson from Three Bridges sent fourteen suggestions, most of them pretty boring, but promised he would display them all on the back of his car. If only he had a car. 'Male stamp collectors need coils.' 'Stamp collectors are never un-hinged', 'Stamp collectors come in mint condition'; 'Stamp Forgeries are a Faking Nuisance'. He also suggested one which many readers sent in, in various forms, none of them really sharp enough, but there is a joke there somewhere, struggling to get out — 'Only stamp collectors have tête-bêche pairs'. His neatest one, for a car window, is 'Stamp collectors don't stop at traffic lights'. Ho, ho.

Tony Torrance of Dollar, which used to be in Clackmannan when I was a boy but is now probably somewhere that's nowhere like Strathclyde, also sent in a slogan which was popular with many people. 'Stamp collectors do it between album covers.'

D. Stables, who never gave a Christian name, which wasn't very friendly, but he or she comes from Betchworth in Surrey, offered some rather smart slogans. 'Swop stamps not wives', 'Stamp collectors lick the world', 'Come on a stamp swopping party' and finished with the simplest one of all — 'Stick to stamps'. Do you like it? Go on, have it. I'm sure David or Derek or Danny or maybe Deirdre or Daphne or Dopey won't mind.

A reader who did reveal her sex, although without enclosing any real proof, wrote from St Helens on Merseyside to suggest

'Join the old soaks — collect stamps'. Thank you, Di Goy, female collector. (Come on, is that your real name?)

G. H. Bishop of Hythe, Kent, sent in one which is so long and dreary I only mention it to save writing to him. 'If life weighs on you heavily in our happy atomic age, make a stamp collection.' Perhaps he's got a very large car?

Thanks to A. Kay of St Helens — good gracious, two stamp collectors in St Helens — for sending in 'Philatelists do it Collectively' and that ever popular 'Stamp Collectors do it between sheets'. A. Rawlinson of Sandiford-on-Thames, Oxford, suggested 'Philatelists do it in their armchair' and 'Philatelists do it se-tenant'.

The rudest slogan was suggested by two people, though with slight variations. John Lamonby, that well-known dealer of Portsmouth, suggested: 'Women are like stamps — they love to be mounted.' While a gentleman from Bridgwater, Somerset, took this idea one stage further, but asked me not to mention his name. 'I'm supposed to be a respectable professional gentleman,' he pleaded. No excuses. They're the worst. Anyway, his attempt is a much subtler slogan with which to bid farewell to the old year. 'Stamp collectors mount, write up and display.' Disgusting.

I have read many columns but none of such high quality as yours. How excellent your words are! I must congratulate you on some truly wonderful sentences.' (M. D. — Carlisle)

A splendid column. You must have all your competitors green with envy.' (B. L. — Fleet Street)

'Keep up the good work. The country needs you.' (M. T. — Downing St.)

Your paragraphs are a work of art. I find your punctuation out of this world. I have learned so much about the English language, thanks to your column.' (A. J. P. T. — Oxford)

'May God bless you for the wonderful inspiration your commas bring to all stamp lovers.' (R. R. — Canterbury)

'Another superb column last week. Everyone here loved it.' (Q. E. — Buckingham Palace)

'What a bargain! What fantastic value! I would gladly pay double for anything else you have.' (S. G. — The Strand)

These are all unsolicited testimonials received during the last two years, all of which I have made up. I guarantee that none of them is true. (Well, the first is. Thanks, Mum.) Money back if you are not satisfied with all the others. Hurry, hurry, while stocks last.

I have been looking through the pages of the stamp press, which of course we all buy for the advertisements. Some of them are hysterical. I laughed till my tweezers hurt, and you can quote me on that! But no, seriously, I find them totally absorbing. Once you get the hang of them, some even make sense. No, hold on. Only joking.

It seems to me, however, that it's not fair. Why should the stamp dealers and auctioneers and the other advertisers have all the fun? Here's us poor hacks, struggling to fill up the gaps between the ads with some deep felt philatelical philosophy or some incredibly abstruse information, while the advertisers can just throw in any old boasts that come to mind or reproduce any old letters, anonymously of course, which tell the world how truly wonderful they are.

At the next meeting of the Philatelic Writers Society I intend to approach the chairman, Major Ronnie Spafford, and put a few proposals to him, or even better, to the glamorous secretary, Hilary Wellsted. I know they won't accept all my suggestions, but we innovators expect to be rebuffed and told not to be so silly, at your age as well. Nonetheless, I intend to bash on and hope that all stamp writers will follow my example. It is high time we stamp writers started pushing our wares and took a few tips from these advertiser johnnies.

'Claim your Discount! Every time you read Hunter at Large you will receive a half price entry to next year's Wembley Exhibition (Caged Birds Show).'

'Get your Golden Key! Send only one hundred copies of this column and we promise you a tatty bit of cardboard worth nothing at all but painted gold which you can keep or throw in the dustbin. Normal price, £8,000.'

'Readers! Your chance to do your own thing! Are you one of those people brimming with creative flair? Why not start your own Business? Your chance to join a course in ten lessons on how to write your very own stamp column! For £5,000 we will send you a Writer's Starter Pack. Genuine used columns, over-matter, libel actions, misprints, screwed-up bits of paper, old ribbons, rejection slips. Plus free waste paper basket!'

'A dream come true? Yes, we have been fortunate in acquiring a large collection of old stamp columns. Totally unsorted! First come, first conned. All GB. These are genuine space fillers. Wide margins, very little thinning, excellent perforations. Your chance to find a classic! Only £1 per kiloware.'

'On Approval! Why not study our stamp columns in the privacy of your home? Send for our Free Catalogue. A unique opportunity to examine the top stamp column in Britain, even before it is published! We can provide words on any old boring subject. All World, GB., Thematic, Rude (Over 18's only). Give us your Wants list. We will do the rest! Money back, if you can find us.'

'£1 off when you read this column. £10 off if you get to the end.'

'Genuine Silk Columns. Commemorative phrases. High values. Definitive articles. Original proofs. Used and unused jokes. All prose in mint condition. Crisp cancellations. Essays, errors, forgeries. Hurry, hurry and buy next week's column. Satisfaction guaranteed. Don't forget to mention Hunter at Large when replying to all advertisements. Thank you.'

The earliest known letters were clay tablets in cuneiform script inserted in clay envelopes and used by court officials and merchants in Asia Minor from 3000 BC.

I'm surprised I have never been prosecuted under the Trades Descriptions Act. All this time, I've completely avoided mentioning it.

Here I am, pretending to be part of *Stamp & Postal History News* and I've never once got round to that sacred topic, postal history. There, I said it. Ha ha, you can't sue me now. I got in first.

For two years I've been chuntering on about my stamp collections, without knowing anything about stamps, so it's about time I wrote about postal history. I don't know anything about that either. But there's a lot of it around.

That's the number one reason for collecting postal history. It's everywhere, available to all, and comes in all sorts of shapes and sizes. The quantity of it out there, just waiting for my hot and eager fingers to rifle through it, which is surely something fingers can't do, what a silly phrase, Hunt. It's staggering anyway.

Secondly, it's cheap. You can get lorry loads of it for very little, well, boxes of it. Compared with stamps, they almost give it away. No wonder all dealers will tell you that postal history as a hobby is booming. Another silly phrase. We stamp people don't boom. Such shy, quiet, retiring folks like us. Let us say that postal history is currently muttering.

Thirdly, it's two-dimensional. Boring old stamps just lie there in the album, or in my case, in drawers and envelopes and in shoe boxes and on shelves and in mysterious cellophane packets with strange hieroglyphics on them which are supposed to tell me who I bought them from, and what the fortune was I paid, but written in my own code so my lady wife never finds out. And now I've forgotten it. Oh what a tangled web we weave when we first practise phil-at-el-lee. See, it scans. Almost.

Postal history usually comes in chunkier bits, larger scraps, with fun on both sides, perhaps several bits of fun, going on all over the place, words and music and pictures. What do stamps do, eh, to earn their keep? So flat and small and square. Goodness knows why I give them house room.

Fourthly, and I hope you're keeping count, but don't worry, you can leave your other hand in your pocket, this is my last number, cucumber. Postal History is personal and unique. Okay, so I've got some Penny Blacks, but so have sixty-eight million other people out there, at least there were sixty-eight million floating around at one time. I certainly haven't got them. Have you searched *everywhere* in your house? Down the side of that sofa?

There's nothing special about a Black, or a Tuppenny Blue. The prices are phenomenal, for good ones, but even so, you don't end up with anything unique. You need to have that draggy old boring old British Guiana 1856 one-cent black on magenta before you can go around boasting to the lads at the next club meeting that you have a unique stamp.

With postal history, you can very quickly build up your own unique collection. Yes, you might say it's unique because no one else in their right mind would want to collect such things. I happen to have the world's best collection of Xmas Cards delivered to this house in 1982. Yup. I have every one. And all the covers intact. No, you can't have any. I've cornered the market and when the right moment arrives, I intend to make a killing. (Remember, they must have *this* address on. See, not as easy as you might think. I bet your boring old Xmas cards have got your address. Who wants them? Drag on the market.)

It's perfectly possible with very little outlay to create something which no one else has got. And occasionally, other people do want them for their collection. A stamp is a stamp is a stamp but postal history has so many permutations and variations and specialisations that you can very soon be all on your own, competing only against yourself. Hence the cheapness and hence the fun of tracking them all down.

What is postal history? Oh, no, you're not going to ask me that, are you? I hate these trick questions. When I became a born-again stamp collector, just three years ago, I met a friend in Carlisle who said he collected postal history and I had no idea what he was talking about. He then explained, and I was even un-wiser.

Postal history, friends, is the study of, oh no, I'm running out of time. You might have asked me earlier. Just let me wander on like that. Right, next time, before your very eyes, I will attempt to define postal history and then, if you are very good, and don't send me any more stamp slogans, I will reveal everything about my own rather wonderful collections of postal history. Watch this space filler . . .

Come to a stamp-swapping party.

What is postal history? I dunno. I'm just an amateur round here, surrounded by clever people with letters after their names. In the last few issues of *Stamp & Postal History News*, I have picked up two definitions of postal history. 'Postal history is the study of routes and rates,' so said one expert. Then in another issue I learned that we should actually call it 'marcophily', which makes it sound like something to do with Princess Anne's husband. In this case it was defined as 'the study of postmarks as a collectable field'.

I'm still no wiser, though older and deeper in debt, which of course is the fate of all amateur stamp collectors and marcophiliacs. Or should it be marcophilics or marcophilists? Postal history is now such a big business that I expect they'll be calling an international conference, just to decide what it is they're doing.

It all sounds so vague. I assumed at first that it meant the history of postage stamps, but judging by those two definitions it means studying routes and postmarks, not stamps. The trouble about the term 'postal history' is that it doesn't imply you actually collect things. They make it appear to be an academic study, an abstract art, rather than the gathering together of real objects. I'm very keen on getting together any real little postal objects, in fact I could even say it is a passion, and I call anything that isn't a stamp, Postal History.

Anyway, while those experts argue amongst themselves, and fall over their BPFs and PHDs and RIPs, come over here, into the light, and I'll let you see some of my postal treasures. Yup, that's my very wonderful collection of postal history to do with Wembley. I started that because I'm interested in football, and stamps, and as we know they go together so neatly. I have most of the different cancellations which were used during the 1924–25 Wembley Exhibition, from the various machines and handstamps, and very pretty they are. I've almost got all the different postcards which were produced by the different national pavilions. Clever old me. All it costs is money. Having told myself that postal history was cheap, I quickly learned that a first day cover for 1925 can cost over £100, which rather alarmed me.

What am I going to do with it all? One of these days, I promise myself I'll sort it out properly and arrange it neatly. I've already got two nice empty albums, the sort they sell at Wembley Stadium today for kids to put their football covers in, and I intend to use them to tell the history of Wembley, postalwise. In the meantime, it's all in a shoe box. I keep on bidding at auctions and picking up things on stalls and ending up with stuff I already have. Anyone want to swap a post card of the Canadian Pavilion by Night?

My collection of Cumbrian postal marks, now that's much better organised. I try to collect different cancellations from as many villages and towns as I can, going back as far as possible.

" I think we ought to get the National Postal Museum on to this ! "

No science in it. But it is very cheap. I can spend hours at stamp fairs, thumbing through the postcard boxes, going all dumb and stupid when I already noticed a faint pencil mark in one corner saying £3 but keeping my finger over it, hoping the bloke will say, okay, 30p. They often do.

Flora, my ten-year-old daughter, bought me six old Cumbrian cards for my birthday. Wasn't that clever of her? She just looked through a pile on a junk stall. Two were good Ambleside cancellations I hadn't got, plus a Penrith, a Keswick and two Carlisles. I'm sure they all have technical names, but I just go for the nice shapes and the age. Real marcopolos could write books on them. Probably have done. That's the nice thing about postal history. Flora could not possibly have managed to pick up six stamps I hadn't got. Every bit of postal history is unique.

Then over here is my brand new collection of Prime Ministerial Postal History. That sounds good, doesn't it? They each consist of free fronts with a nice 'Free' cancellation on each, one signed by Melbourne and one signed by Gladstone. I knew you'd be excited. Okay, you can call it autograph hunting if you like, but the postal markings are all there. Yes, that's true, I only have two so far. Don't be mean. Two's a collection, isn't it? Listen, I intend to call my own international conference soon, then we'll soon settle all these arguments. That's the best thing of all about postal history. We're our own experts.

"It's the latest thing - special handstamp tattoos!"

I have a new Saturday morning passion, almost as passionate as the Saturday morning children's cinema shows I used to go to. 'We are the boys and girls well known as, Minors of the ABC.' Ah, that tune still comes back to me, down all the days.

I've just discovered these amazing stalls under the arches of Charing Cross Bridge. That's beside the Embankment, in London, England, Europe, the World. You must have heard of London before. It's always on television.

I take my daughter Flora to a dancing class every Saturday morning in Covent Garden and I have an hour to fill in, just hanging about. I usually take a look at Gibbons, having a keen interest in all members of the animal family, then the delightful dealers in the International Stamp Centre. (They're always moaning about bad publicity, so there you are lads, ten per cent off next time. Thanks.)

Last Saturday I chanced to wander further afield, across the Strand, and I came to a row of stalls under a bridge, full of coin people and old army stuff, all very interesting, but I have enough worries in life with stamps to start collecting anything else. One of the blokes said that further along, just beside the tube, I would find lots of real stamp stalls.

They took me a while to find, as that part of London at weekends is full of non-Londoners, staggering around between those horrible hamburger places and smelly caffs, sitting in windows, wondering where they are and why they have come to London, England, oh do get on with it.

I eventually found them and there before me were rows and rows of stalls, selling old newspapers, army badges, uniforms, postcards, magazines and yes, a great many stamp stalls as well. I felt like Aladdin shouting Eureka when he had discovered Archimedes' principle.

All this going on and I never knew anything about it. Isn't life wonderful? I feasted my tired, old eyes, not knowing where to begin, then very slowly I started working my way down, vowing not to look across at any other stalls till I had exhausted the first row.

I do regularly buy at the International Stamp Centre, world famous for their delightful stamp shops (that must be twenty per cent now), and Mr Gibbons has oft had the pleasure of my company and my cheque book, but they sell mainly high-class stuff. What I'm looking for in life is a load of old rubbish. I just want to scratch around, finger all the packets, thumb through the jumble, leaf through the tat, be allowed to get on with it and feel no compulsion actually to buy any of the old junk, though I always do.

I do know various street markets where there's often one stamp stall, but that's no sport and very often they never turn up. I have gone to those fairs they hold in hotels on the first Sunday after the tenth Saturday in every third month, but I have a block about them. I dunno what it is. Call it meanness if you like. They always seem so expensive. I don't like the central heating, the plush carpets, the hotel atmosphere. With a scruffy old stall, out in the open air, you can convince yourself There Be Bargains Here.

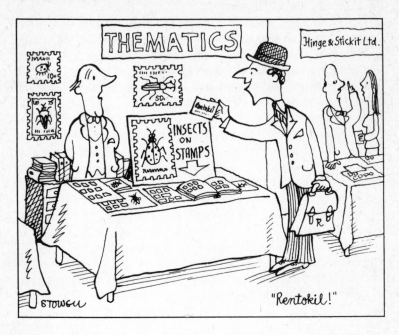

So, to discover twenty open-air scruffy stalls all selling stamps or postcards, which is what my greedy eyes worked out, well, it was bliss to be alive and to be a stamp collector was very heaven.

Now, what did I buy? Let's see. I have before me four very lovely railway postcards showing interiors of royal coaches, a passing whim which relieved me of £3. He wanted £4 but I got £1 off. Wow. There's nothing quite like the joy of saving money by spending it on things you never knew you wanted to spend it on.

Yes, and here is a Penny Black I got for £6, beating him down from £7. What a pro I am. Don't look too carefully at that bite out of the top. If you don't mention it I won't. Just look at these letters. EK. Yup, one more for my reconstruction. Did I tell you about this? Oh, sorry. Several times. It's a lifetime's project, you see. I aim to re-create a whole sheet, 240 stamps, any plates, any condition, as long as they're not more than £15 each. (And I pay cash. Quick. Have a look amongst your rubbish.) I've got about thirty so far. Next week we're going on bread and dripping.

I had to rush away at one o'clock, so I didn't get much, to pick up Flora from her dance class. As I got to the end of that first row, I realised there were another forty stalls, through an archway into a garage. I hadn't known they were there. I might have got Penny Blax cheaper, or nicer royal trains, or even better rubbish.

I'll never sleep this week. Roll on Saturday.

Stamp collectors lick the world.

I was wandering round the stamp stalls under Charing Cross Bridge last week, my new Saturday morning taste thrill, when I recognised a familiar face.

There are quite a few well-known people who are stamp collectors. Adam Faith, James Prior, the Queen, Hammond Innes, Chay Blyth and others.

I've never seen any of them hunting through the rubbish on the stamp stalls I patronise. Perhaps they're closet collectors, or send their butler out with a shopping bag.

This familiar face was not buying stamps, or even turning over all the junk, or poking through the old shoe boxes. He was behind a counter, selling stamps, a real live dealer. That's something you don't catch the Queen doing.

It was David Benedictus, the distinguished novelist. You must remember his first novel, *The Fourth of June*, set at Eton, which was a best-seller. He's done about a dozen more novels since then, including *The Rabbi's Wife*, and also a couple of books on antiques. I knew he was a keen collector of antiques and stuff because I used to enjoy his weekly column on collecting in the *Standard*. But I never knew he was interested in stamps. Join the club. Rather raises the tone of my Saturday mornings, buying rubbish, I mean rather wonderful bargain stamps, from an Old Etonian.

He's been running a stall once a month at Cookham for years, just for fun and a bit of pocket money, selling mainly books and china. 'It has become much harder to buy job lots cheaply. What I always used to go for in auctions was "Trunk and Contents". It was always more expensive to buy at country auctions, but London was very cheap, until recently. The price of buying in has gone up but not the selling price on stalls.'

He has sold occasional stamp collections over the years, job lots found in trunks, and noticed that they seemed to be doing much better than his china and other bits. So he decided to concentrate on stamps for once, just to give it a try. Last week, when I chanced to see him, happened to be his first day ever running a stamp stall.

He had invested £1,000 to stock his stall, buying four general collections at an auction at Phillips. The main collection was All World, two contained modern commemorative covers and another was Oceania. Since his schooldays, he has always liked New Zealand stamps. 'They're so pretty.'

He'd had a poor morning till I arrived, worrying if he should let odd stamps go when they were part of a set, yet thinking 20p is 20p and he's got to sell something. I was the first of the big spenders. I lashed out and bought some commem. covers, all at half catalogue price, and spent £8.50 in all. Well, he was an old friend.

Then a bloke beside me, encouraged by my largesse, paid £25 for a French stamp. David didn't know whether it was a good one or not. He just sold it for a tenth of the catalogue price, which was what the man offered. By the end of the day, so he said when I rang him later, he had sold £100 of stamps. Not bad. Or was it?

His stall had cost him £8 then there was £1 for parking. For a day's writing work, doing a profile for *Radio Times*, which he was about to do the next day, then he can obviously make a great deal more money with his pen. Writing novels, however, is not all that well paid, and writing novels is what he likes to do best of all.

'On my old stall, selling china and books, I always reckoned in my mind to take in ten per cent of my stock value in a day. So having paid out £1,000 for my stamps, £100 a day was not bad.'

It still seems like hard work to me. It's going to take him ten days' work, spread over ten weeks, just to get his money back.

'Yes, but it was my first day. People have to know I'm here. Quite a few said they would come back next week. Now I don't know whether to invest in more stamps or not. My GB is very poor and people didn't seem to think much of the stamps I think are very pretty. They all wanted countries I didn't think were popular — such as Saudi Arabia and Indian States.'

And what did you think of us, David? Hmm? We poor miserable punters, grey faces in our old raincoats, bending over your stall, fingering through your precious stock, muttering to ourselves, then asking for ridiculous things you can't possibly carry?

'Well, compared with running a china stall, which is usually very jolly, stamp collectors seem a bit serious. They're all very repressed and I think that some of them . . .'

Careful, David. You don't want your first week to be your last week . . .

Stamp collectors come in mint condition.

I got a present in the post this morning. I was hoping it might be a large bribe from some stamp dealer, trying to make sure I would be nice to him from now on. Fat chance, on either possibility. Naturally, I would never allow my art to be compromised.

I often wonder why I write about stamps when there are just so few perks in this funny old field. When I was a woman's editor, come on, you must remember when I did the 'Look' pages in the *Sunday Times*, they were terribly good, I was once sent a complete set of underpants — one for all the men in the office, which meant I got the lot. Then when I was Atticus, my goodness, the free lunches I used to gobble. Even when I wrote a sports column in *The Times* I used to get free tickets to Spurs.

I also got free tickets to Arsenal. You have to take the rough with the even rougher.

Show-business writers, they get flown round the world all the time, put up at the best hotels, wined and dined. The only drawback there is that you have to actually talk to the show-business stars. Television critics, those clever clogs in your morning and Sunday newspapers, have special lunch-time screenings laid on for them, plus drinks and goodies to make them enjoy the shows even more. It means they can have their evenings free instead of having to watch boring old TV.

Since arriving in stamps, let me see, I do now get a free ticket for the big stamp shows, but that's because I'm a member of the

" Wavy line cancellation to missing phosphor – any good stamp shops round here?"

Philatelic Writers Society. Fully paid up as well. The Crown Agents do send me samples of their new stamps, for which I'm terribly grateful, thanks lads. Imagine the British Post Office letting you have anything for free. I must spend a fortune on all their issues and presentation packs, which does mean I feel absolutely free to rubbish them. New stamps, being a licence to print money, don't cost them much. I'm still waiting for some old Penny Blacks or some nice Wembley material. That would really be a test of the stamp world's generosity — and my moral conscience.

They're all so hard up in the stamp world, that's the problem, or so they say. I've bought several dealers drinks in my time but I can't remember getting many back, oh no, I tell a lie, one day in Covent Garden in the International Stamp Centre Malcolm Sprei did give me a plastic cup of milky coffee. It was rather lukewarm. I suspect he'd ordered one too many by mistake, in his mad, impulsive, spendthrift way, and I just happened to turn up. Lucky me.

I am not touting for freebies, just observing that compared with other specialist journalists one gets little help, of any sort, from the trade. Apart from Stanley Gibbons, who have a very good press officer, the stamp world has no idea how to even send out information about itself. Sob, sob. I know you don't give a fig. Let them eat plastic.

So I tore open this interesting-looking package with alacrity. We don't have a paper-knife in our house. It was from an American gentleman called William A. Dyer Jr., President of Indianapolis Star. He said he was a reader of my stuff and this was just a little present.

'As a gesture of appreciation I'm sending you a postage stamp tie from the Smithsonian Institution. It might prove a conversation piece at philatelic gatherings. The stamp pictured is the 1918 error of a 24-cent airmail in which the biplane was inverted. One hundred were issued. They're rather rare and valuable.'

I'm sure he means the stamp is rare and valuable, not the tie, though it is a very nice one. I've often wondered what to talk about at philatelic gatherings, apart from where's the drink? The only trouble is that I don't wear ties. I gave them up when I stopped going out to work and retired, exhausted, to work at home on my books.

We have a family wedding soon, so I'll stun the relations by buying a suit, just to show off my amusing philatelic tie. It's in Surrey so if you happen to be there, look out for me. I won't be the one standing on my head. It will be the upside down stamp on my tie.

Stamp dealers get perforated ulcers.

Ever since I got the tie, though, I've been wondering what to send in return. I'm sure William A. Dyer Jr. doesn't expect anything. It was simply a wonderful, spontaneous gesture. I do have that effect on people. Why, the VAT people send me letters and booklets every day, without me ever asking them.

I've got to think of something philatelic in return. But what does one give to stamp collectors, especially when they are strangers and one doesn't know their special interests? Hmm? Quite a problem.

The stamp world as a whole is very poor on stamp merchandising, compared with other fields. Football fans have piles of junk to chose from, badges and tee-shirts and stickers and hats and bags and jumpers and last week I even saw ladies' knickers with the Spurs cockerell crest emblazoned on them. In a window in Tottenham, I hasten to add, not in the flesh.

Beatles fans, they had it so easy, though these days all that Sixties Beatle tat is impossible to get and costs a fortune. Hold on to any Beatle wigs you might have, stashed away on the back of your head. Or if you have any *Beatle Monthlies*, let me know. I'm a few short for my collection. Bird fans, they seem to do very well, and that Goodie Bill Oddy is always on the radio and TV going on about his bird-watching habits. There's even a bird-spotting book in the bestseller list at the moment. We must have as many stamp fans as those bird fans, yet what is our trade doing to keep us in the public mind and at the front of the counter? Not much, as far as I have ever seen.

So I went to have a look at Stanley Gibbons' new and very marvellous shop in the Strand to see what rubbish — I mean treasures — they have for sale for the stamp collector who has everything. I didn't want stamps, thank you very much, or accessories, but dafter things, souvenirs and such.

I bought a Penny Black badge, a bargain already at only 75p, but I wondered if it might be a trifle modest to send all the way to my penfriend, William Dyer, in Indianapolis. After all, he had sent me a rather expensive tie.

I thought about a pair of Penny Black cufflinks, at £1.75, or a Penny Black tie-pin at £1.75, or a Penny Black notebook at £1.75. Penny Black seems to be the only motif they can think of. They did sell ties a few years ago, with a Cape Triangular on them, but no more. Dan Cooke, the shop manager, says that the badges are his best seller. But on the whole, there is not a big demand for stamp merchandising. They occasionally have stamp wrapping paper, at 25p a sheet, but not that day.

It's children who mostly buy stamp souvenirs, especially the Penny Black badges. The cufflinks and tie pins are of course sexist and adultist and don't have such a following. Certainly not.

I have seen people wearing various stamp ties at stamp meetings, but I think they are mainly sold by societies to their members. Anyway, that would be copying. I had to think of something different. We stamp fans, even though we are supposedly four million strong, we don't seem to be catered for at all.

Then I noticed that though his letter head said he was called William Dyer, he had actually signed himself Bill Dyer. Phew, what a relief. I rushed to my special album of Penny Reds, all cheapos and nasties, but arranged under their different letters. I found quite a nice one lettered BD. Finding one with the letters WD would of course have been impossible as they didn't reach that far down the alphabet.

So I'm putting it in the post today, the perfect individual present for any stamp collector. I hope his eyesight is up to recognising the letters, but I have displayed it nicely. I'm keeping the Penny Black badge, all for myself. We children.

He's so vulgar, he always goes for the lowest common denominations.

After four years as a born-again stamp collector, four years of joy and tears before the mast, four years of serious fun out of something I had not done since childhood, I achieved the ultimate accordian. I was asked to speak about my hobby. Yup.

It was from the Finchley and District Philatelic Society that the call came. Founded 1943, very thriving, over 150 members, very influential in the London Borough of Barnet, you must have heard of them. I said yes months earlier, thinking that when the time came I would be bound to know *something* about stamps.

They asked me what I would like to talk about and I didn't know what to say. I must have muttered that I would just get my stuff down from where I keep it and try to talk about it for as long as possible, perhaps even for five minutes. Through the post came their programme for the year, printed on pink card, full of impressive-sounding collectors down to talk about impressive things like 'Earth Science on Stamps', 'Icelandic Postal History' and 'Luxembourg Covers'. There was me, billed under the heading 'Some Stamps from my Lavatory Wall and How They Came to Be There'.

I still hoped they might forget about it, that philatelic life might manage to go on in Finchley without me, but the week before the Big Day, the Secretary, Alan Drake, rang to check that I was still alive, had not emigrated, and would I like dinner with him beforehand.

Three days previously I had spoken at the Cambridge Union for which I did no preparation whatsoever, and I was rotten, so I decided for my second, and final, public performance of this year I better do some homework. I toured the lavatories — all three of them, pleasure mad in our house — and got down my Penny Reds with the family's initials on, the Penny Blacks with my initials on, the Numbers inside Maltese Crosses, the Royal Commemorative Stamps, the World Cups in Stamps and a whole host of other treasures, all of them absolutely covered in dust.

I hadn't looked at most of them for three years, not since I first put them up to amaze the family and excite visitors. That was the intention. On a rough estimate, I realised I could only talk about each of them for two minutes. Such simple things I collected, such naive assemblies, how young and green I was when all this madness first started, back in 1979.

I have since started one good collection, one on which I have spent a fortune, and this is my Wembley Exhibition stuff. But how can I show it? Mr Drake had mentioned in his letter that they would provide 8 frames, whatever that means. He made it sound like a gardening competition.

Most of my Wembley material was still in shoe-boxes, drawers and even the envelopes in which it had arrived from the auctions. Well, it could give me a pretext, at long last, to get it into some sort of shape.

I stayed up half the night before the meeting, just trying to shove all my precious covers and cards and stamps inside any old bits of plastic bags I could find. I didn't have time to label most of it. A poor thing, but mine own.

I was given a very nice dinner beforehand, by Mr Drake and his wife, melon with a cherry on top, chicken with a slice of pineapple, and then I saw his collections. I counted over fifty albums, all in immaculate order, all beautifully arranged, and I wondered whether I should jump out the window and run away. He would probably have tracked me down. Before he retired, Mr Drake used to be a private investigator.

The hall was crowded, with a very good turn-out, and I managed to spin out my assorted wall collections for about half an hour, then we had a break. It had gone *reasonably* well, not Gold Medal standard, not worthy of an Oscar, but I don't think anybody fell asleep.

After the break, I went into the serious stuff, all about the history of the Wembley Exhibition, illustrated with my material. Several members had actually been there, back in 1924, but they were too polite to correct any of my errors.

Actually talking about my stamps, for the first time in my life, helped to clear my mind. I recommend it to all collectors. I began to see patterns and themes and how, given time, I could arrange my stuff. My scruffy old plastic covers, all in different shapes and sizes, amused them, but they did seem to like the contents and I got some good hints on how I should display them in future.

If there is a future? And why not. Despite what some members of this family might think, and I'm mentioning no names, I have not after all wasted the last four years. It has given me a lot of pleasure. I intend to go on.

They gave me a printed scroll afterwards, just to prove I exhibited before their Society. So there. Something else for the albums. Roll on the next four years.

"Look Dad! I've swopped your stamp with the spelling mistake on it for a perfectly good one!"

Stamp collectors get medals for it.

The cover they tried to ban . . .

No, your eyes are not playing tricks on you. Opposite *is* a different version of the drawing which is on the cover of this book. It is the work of Wally Fawkes, better known as 'Trog', the famous and prize-laden cartoonist who works for the *Observer* and also draws Flook in the *Daily Mail*. I hope I can trust *you* to behave in a decent fashion and not react in a disgusting way . . .

Wally Fawkes kindly agreed to do the cover for the book, and came up with this idea. It shows me so carried away with the Joy of Stamps that I am totally ignoring the more ordinary, mundane pleasures of life — such as wine, women and song — which are being offered through the window. Good idea, huh?

I thought so, but when it was shown to a few distinguished members of the philatelic world they said no, certainly not, tut tut, we in stamps don't want that sort of thing. Half-naked girls? How disgusting. It is bad enough that you're trying to launch a so-called *funny* book on innocent stamp-collectors, who have never had such a thing before, but decent philatelists will on no account buy a book with a hussy on the front. Please take it away and alter it . . .

Ah, well. Wally, being a gentleman — and also a brilliant jazz clarinettist, did you know that? — took it away and drew a more refined background, the one you see on the front. I thought you should be told.

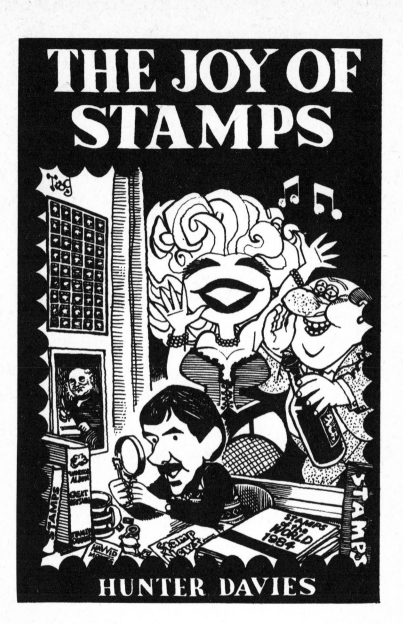

Philatelist's Alphabet

(Geoffrey Mansell of Queniborough, Leicester, found this alphabet in an old stamp catalogue. Perhaps he should have left it there.)

A   is for Album, which we must keep dry,

B   is for Booklets, of stamps we can buy.

C   is for Cancels, much rarer when fine,

D   is for Die-plate, or even design.

E   is for Essays, and Entires as well,

F   is for Fakes, that the Forgers sell.

G   is the Gauge, for perforate measure,

H   is for Hobby, we do at our leisure.

I   is for Inverted, a watermark trait,

J   is for Jubilee, edge-lining a plate.

K   is for Key-type and also for King,

L   is for Line-perf and our Lettering.

M   is for Margin it's usually a border,

N   is for Names of Countries in order.

O   is for Officials, a special design,

P   is for Post-Due, a Post Office fine.

Q   is for Quadrille, feint tiny squares,

R   is for Reprints and also Repairs.

S   is for Spaces for sets incomplete,

T   is for Thematic, a stamp-story neat.

U   is for Used, the fine ones are better,

V   is for Valid or Valuable letter.

W   is for Wants-list to dealer's domain,

X   is for Kiss-stamp found on a pane.

Y   is for Yvert, a foreign-stamp saga,

Z   is for Zanzibar and end of this page.

Definitive Ending

The philatelist stood at the golden gates,
His head bowed very low,
And sadly he said to the Man of Fates:
'Which way have I to go?'
'What hast thou done?' St Peter asked,
'To gain admission here?'
'I've plated Penny Reds and Blacks,
For many and many a year.'
'A GB fan,' St Peter gasped
And he gently pressed a bell;
'Step right inside and pick your harp —
You've had your share of Hell.'

"I just wondered if you might have a special 'Pearly Gates' handstamp?"

Thanks for stamp slogans, and other comments, used to brighten up this book, to . . .

B. N. Ridley, Leeds,
Di Goy, St Helens
A. Rawlinson, Sandford on Thames
A. Kay, St Helens
Colin Wilson, Crawley
Tony Torrance, Dollar
D. Stables, Bletchworth
J. M. Brown, Banbury
D. P. Turner, Bridgwater
G. D. Findlay, Tayside
Pat Walder, Isle of Wight
Irene Lawford, Kenton
Roy Hollans, Chester
John Manners, Paisley